RUSSIA 2016 HUMAN RIGHTS REPORT

EXECUTIVE SUMMARY

The Russian Federation has a highly centralized, authoritarian political system dominated by President Vladimir Putin. The bicameral Federal Assembly consists of a directly elected lower house (State Duma) and an appointed upper house (Federation Council), both of which lacked independence from the executive. State Duma elections during 2016 and the presidential election in 2012 were marked by accusations of government interference and manipulation of the electoral process.

Security forces generally reported to civilian authorities, except in some areas of the North Caucasus.

The continuing occupation and purported "annexation" of Ukraine's Crimean Peninsula continued to affect the human rights situation significantly and negatively. The government continued to train, equip, and supply pro-Russian forces in eastern Ukraine, who were joined by numerous fighters from Russia. Credible observers attributed thousands of civilian deaths and injuries, as well as widespread abuses, to Russian-backed separatists in Ukraine's Donbas region, and to Russian occupation authorities in Crimea (see the *Country Reports on Human Rights* for Ukraine). Authorities also conducted politically motivated arrests, detentions, and trials of Ukrainian citizens in Russia, many of whom claimed to have been tortured. Human rights groups asserted that numerous Ukrainian citizens remained in Russia as political prisoners.

The most significant human rights problems were:

Restrictions on Political Participation and Freedom of Expression, Assembly, and Media: Authorities restricted citizens' ability to choose their government through free and fair elections and increasingly instituted a range of measures to suppress dissent. The government passed repressive laws and selectively employed existing ones to harass, discredit, prosecute, imprison, detain, fine, and suppress individuals and organizations critical of the government. Amendments to antiterrorism laws, known as the "Yarovaya package," granted authorities sweeping powers. Authorities especially targeted individuals and organizations that professed support for the government of Ukraine or opposed the Russian government's activities in Ukraine.

Suppression of Civil Society: Authorities further stymied the work of nongovernmental organizations (NGOs) through the "foreign agents" and "undesirable foreign organization" laws. Authorities also significantly expanded the definition of political activities to bring more NGOs under the "foreign agents" category. Authorities began fining NGOs for not disclosing "foreign agent" status, while courts closed NGOs for violations involving the foreign agents' list. Under the expanded definition of political activities, authorities added environmental and HIV-prevention organizations to the list.

Government Discrimination against Minorities: Authorities continued to discriminate against members of some religious and ethnic minorities; lesbian, gay, bisexual, transgender, and intersex (LGBTI) persons; and migrant workers. The Yarovaya package restricted "missionary activity," including preaching, proselytizing, disseminating religious materials, or engaging in interfaith discussion; authorities used it to harass religious minorities. Authorities utilized a law prohibiting "propaganda" of nontraditional sexual relations to minors to harass the LGBTI community.

Other problems included allegations of torture and excessive force by law enforcement officers that sometimes led to deaths; prison overcrowding, and substandard and life-threatening prison conditions; executive branch pressure on the judiciary; lack of due process in politically motivated cases; electoral irregularities; extensive official corruption; violence against women; limits on women's rights; trafficking in persons; discrimination against persons with disabilities; social stigma against persons with HIV/AIDS; and limitations on workers' rights.

The government failed to take adequate steps to prosecute or punish most officials who committed abuses, resulting in a climate of impunity.

Conflict in the North Caucasus between government forces, insurgents, Islamist militants, and criminals led to numerous abuses, including killings, torture, physical abuse, politically motivated abductions, and a general degradation in the rule of law. Ramzan Kadyrov's government in Chechnya generally did not investigate or prosecute abuses, and security forces committed abuses with impunity.

Section 1. Respect for the Integrity of the Person, Including Freedom from:

a. Arbitrary Deprivation of Life and other Unlawful or Politically Motivated Killings

There were several reports that the government or its agents committed arbitrary or unlawful killings. In the North Caucasus, both authorities and local militants reportedly carried out numerous extrajudicial killings (see section 1.g.).

Prison officials and police allegedly subjected inmates and suspects in custody to physical abuse that in some instances resulted in death (see section 1.c., Prison and Detention Center Conditions). On July 15, police in Ingushetia separately questioned Marem Daliyeva and her husband Magomed Daliyev for suspected involvement in a bank robbery. During the interrogation law enforcement officials insulted and threatened Daliyeva, then covered her head in a black bag, and took her to an undisclosed location for further questioning. They continued to hit her and administered electric shock to her hands and her abdomen. They returned her to the police station and held her for an additional two hours before she was released and learned that her husband had died during his questioning. As a result of complaints filed by Daliyeva, on July 19 the Investigative Committee opened a criminal case on exceeding authority and violating the rights of a citizen. As of August 12, the investigation had not yet determined responsibility for Daliyev's death or treatment during interrogation.

Physical abuse continued to be a problem in the armed forces. While there were no clear examples of physical abuse leading to death, there were cases of suspicious deaths. In one example, commanding officers deemed the death of conscript Andrey Shlychkov in March a suicide in their official account. The family claimed that senior officers beat the conscript to death, and then hanged him to suggest a suicide. The family claimed that accounts from fellow conscripts and bruising on Shlychkov's body supported this version. The Committee for the Social Protection of Servicemen in Bashkiriya was investigating the cause of death, and a criminal investigation into whether the case involved instigation to suicide was underway.

In February 2015 opposition politician Boris Nemtsov, deputy prime minister during the administration of Boris Yeltsin, was shot and killed on the streets of Moscow near the Kremlin. Authorities ultimately arrested five Chechens for the crime, with an additional suspect killed in an attempt to apprehend him in Chechnya. On October 3, the jury trial of the suspects began in a military court, with all five of the defendants pleading not guilty. One of the defendants, Zaur Dadayev, was formerly deputy commander of the North battalion of the Interior

Troops of the Ministry of Internal Affairs in Chechnya. Reports indicated that Dadayev might have held a position within the ministry at the time of the killing. Dadayev confessed to the killing before recanting, claiming he had been tortured while in detention. He implied that he had received orders for Nemtsov's killing from Ruslan Geremeyev, another officer who served in the North battalion. The court summoned Geremeyev to testify as a witness on December 13, but Geremeyev did not appear in court. Russian authorities were unable to identify Geremeyev's whereabouts. In December 2015 investigators charged Dadayev, Anzor Gubashev, Khamzat Bakhayev, Shadid Gubashev, and Temirlan Eskerkhanov with committing the murder as part of an organized group and illegally purchasing, carrying, transporting, and storing firearms.

The country played a significant military role in conflicts outside of its borders, in Syria and in eastern Ukraine, where human rights organizations attributed thousands of civilian deaths as well as other human rights abuses to Russian-backed separatists and Russian occupation authorities in Crimea (see *Country Reports on Human Rights* for Ukraine). Since September 2015 the country has conducted military operations including airstrikes in the continuing conflict in Syria. According to human rights organizations, the country's forces have taken actions such as bombing urban areas and humanitarian aid convoys during the conflict, including purposefully targeting civilians (see *Country Reports on Human Rights* for Syria).

In January a British public inquiry into the death in 2006 of Alexander Litvinenko, a former secret police (KGB) officer turned whistleblower and Putin critic, concluded that two Russian nationals, Andrey Lugovoy and Dmitriy Kuvtun, poisoned Litvinenko with a rare radioactive isotope, polonium 210, in London. The report also found it was probable that President Putin and the Federal Security Service (FSB) chief at the time, Nikolay Patrushev, had approved the killing, which was likely an FSB operation.

b. Disappearance

Enforced disappearances for both political and financial reasons continued in the North Caucasus (see section 1.g.). According to the 2016 report of the UN Working Group on Enforced or Involuntary Disappearances, there were 480 outstanding cases of enforced or involuntary disappearances in the country.

Security forces were allegedly responsible for the kidnapping and disappearance of asylum seekers from Central Asia, particularly Uzbekistan and Tajikistan (see section 2.d.).

c. Torture and Other Cruel, Inhuman, or Degrading Treatment or Punishment

Although the constitution prohibits such practices, numerous credible reports indicated that law enforcement personnel engaged in torture, abuse, and violence to coerce confessions from suspects, and authorities generally did not hold officials accountable for such actions. If law enforcement officers were prosecuted, they were typically charged with simple assault or exceeding their authority. According to human rights activists, judges often elected instead to use laws against abuse of power, because this definition, according to legal statutes, better captures the difference in authority between an officer of the law and the private individual who was abused.

There were reports of deaths as a result of torture (see section 1.a.).

Physical abuse of suspects by police officers was reportedly systemic and usually occurred within the first few days of arrest. Reports from human rights groups and former police officers indicated that police most often used electric shocks, suffocation, and stretching or applying pressure to joints and ligaments because those methods were considered less likely to leave visible marks. In the North Caucasus, local law enforcement organizations as well as federal security services reportedly committed torture (see section 1.g.).

In one example, on November 1, the independent news outlet *Meduza* published a letter written by jailed activist Ildar Dadin to his wife alleging that he and other inmates were being systematically tortured and threatened with death if they tried to complain. As of November 3, the head of the IK-7 prison in Segezha where Dadin was held, Sergey Kossiyev, had reportedly resigned, and the federal Investigative Committee announced that prosecutors had been sent to the prison to look into the allegations. Presidential spokesman Dmitriy Peskov said the allegations deserved "very close attention" and that President Putin would be informed about the matter. In 2015 Dadin was the first person to be convicted under a new legal provision that criminalizes repeated violations of the law on public events (see section 2.b).

Authorities reportedly tortured defendants and witnesses involved in high-profile trials. Ukrainians Mykola Karpyuk and Stanislav Klikh, convicted on May 26 for participating in military activities against Russian armed forces during the conflict in Chechnya in the 1990s, claimed that statements they made during the investigation were made under torture. According to Karpyuk authorities also threatened to kidnap and torture his son.

Arrests and court decisions related to police torture continued to come from the Republic of Tatarstan. On June 18, authorities arrested Nazilya Gainatullina, the head of the training department in the local federal penitentiary service in Tatarstan, for exceeding authority with the use of force. This arrest arose as a result of video footage released from a Kazan prison showing convicted criminals standing facing a wall while being hit by police officers.

Police and individuals operating with the tacit approval of authorities conducted attacks on political and human rights activists, critics of government policies, and persons linked to the opposition.

On March 9, a group of masked men beat two members of the Committee for the Prevention of Torture and six journalists traveling with them on a reporting tour between Ingushetia and Chechnya. The journalists included a Norwegian, a Swede, and six Russians, two of whom were human rights activists. According to Human Rights Watch (HRW), at least 15 men stopped the minibus carrying the eight persons and their driver. The attackers burned the group's minibus. All were injured, and five were hospitalized. No one has been prosecuted for the attack. While a government spokesperson called the attack "unacceptable," HRW reported that "authorities' utter failure to hold anyone to account" gave a green light to further attacks.

On March 16 in Chechnya, a mob of unidentified individuals attacked human rights defender Igor Kalyapin, head of the Committee for the Prevention of Torture. They hit him and threw eggs, antiseptic liquid, and flour on him. Local authorities investigated the attack but never filed charges.

Reports by refugees, NGOs, and the press suggested a pattern of police carrying out beatings, arrests, and extortions of persons whose ethnic makeup was assumed to be Romani, Central Asian, African, or of a Caucasus nationality.

There were multiple reports of authorities' detaining defendants for psychiatric evaluations for up to 30 days as a means of pressuring them or sending them for psychiatric treatment as a means of punishing them. On May 6, authorities forcibly removed Voronezh activist Dmitriy Vorobyovskiy from his home and took him to a psychiatric hospital where they tied him to a bed for three hours and injected him with unknown substances, according to his attorney. He remained in the hospital and has not yet been brought before a judge; no charges have been filed. Human rights groups called for his release, noting that his detention appeared linked to his frequent protests in Voronezh against the government and in support of political prisoners.

Nonlethal physical abuse and hazing continued to be a problem in the armed forces, although violations related to hazing in the military were fewer than in previous years. The NGO Union of Committees of Soldiers' Mothers confirmed that a decrease of incidents of "dedovshchina" (a pattern of hazing) in 2015 continued into 2016.

In March 2015 the St. Petersburg City Court found that military commissioners violated recruits' rights by not taking into account their medical files. There were continued problems with recruits medically unfit for duty being forced to enter into the army. NGOs reported complaints from conscripts drafted into service despite their claims of poor health. Soldiers returning from fighting in Ukraine also complained to NGOs of obstacles in receiving health care, because medical files had not been kept. Suicide among recruits continued to be a problem.

Prison and Detention Center Conditions

Conditions in prisons and detention centers varied but were sometimes harsh and life threatening. Overcrowding, abuse by guards and inmates, limited access to health care, food shortages, and inadequate sanitation were common in prisons, penal colonies, and other detention facilities.

<u>Physical Conditions</u>: Authorities held prisoners and detainees in the following types of facilities: temporary police detention centers, pretrial detention facilities, correctional labor colonies (ITKs), prisons (including prisons for those who violate ITK rules), medical correctional facilities, and educational labor colonies for juveniles. Correctional colonies varied according to security regime, from light to maximum security. Unofficial prisons, many of which were located in the North Caucasus, reportedly continued to operate. While the penal code establishes the separation of women and men, juveniles and adults, and pretrial detainees and convicts into separate quarters, there was anecdotal evidence that not all prison facilities followed these rules.

Prison overcrowding remained a serious problem. Although the federal minimum standard of space per person in detention is 26 square feet, Presidential Human Rights Council member Andrey Babushkin reported in October 2015 that inmates were being confined to spaces far below the mandatory minimum, particularly in prison facilities in larger cities. As of the end of 2015, according to the Prosecutor General's Office, 54 pretrial detention facilities in 24 regions of the country did not provide detainees the mandatory amount of space. The situation was particularly concerning in pretrial detention facilities in Moscow. As of December 2015, all facilities in Moscow were crowded beyond capacity and seven of them were overextended by 27 percent. The size of the country's prison population exacerbated the overcrowding. According to the most recent data available, prisons were operating at approximately 95 percent of capacity in 2014, up from 90 percent in 2013.

Penal Reform International reported conditions were generally better in women's colonies than in men's but remained substandard. Thirteen women's facilities also contained facilities for underage children of inmates who had no options for housing them with friends or relatives.

On April 27, Prosecutor General Yuriy Chayka announced that in 2015 approximately 4,000 individuals died in prison facilities and that the overwhelming majority of deaths were related to poor medical care. According to his report, 87 percent of deaths related to various diseases.

In the first six months of the year, 49 persons died in police stations, pretrial detention, or temporary detention, according to a tally maintained by the website *Russian Ebola*. Causes of death included medical conditions, suicide, and injuries sustained while in detention. In the second quarter of the year, 20 detainees died, nine of whom died in police stations, seven in temporary detention centers, and four in investigative detention. Of these deaths, authorities attributed nine to suicide and seven to "sudden deterioration of health." The remaining four died from a beating, a fire, an injury sustained while committing a crime, and torture, respectively.

The majority of deaths in prison and pretrial detention were reportedly related to a lack of quality care, according to a study conducted under the auspices of a presidential grant. A member of the monitoring commission conducting the study stated that the majority of prisoners' illnesses were associated with the detention environment, citing an example of a holding cell in a Krasnodar district court where the walls were covered in fungus and there was no ventilation.

In April a cancer-stricken female prison inmate in St. Petersburg died awaiting implementation of a European Court of Human Rights (ECHR) ruling ordering her transfer to a civil hospital. This was the second such death case in St. Petersburg. The ECHR found that the prison hospital did not provide adequate medical care, but a local district court refused to approve the transfer. At least three additional female cancer sufferers were in the prison hospital; two of them had similar ECHR transfer orders. On July 13, a 55-year-old prisoner, Nikolay Khozyashev, reportedly committed suicide in a penitentiary facility in Perm because prison officials were not providing medical assistance.

In the case of Sergey Magnitsky, a lawyer who died of medical neglect and abuse while in pretrial detention in 2009, authorities had not, as of year's end, brought those reportedly responsible for his death to justice. The investigation into the circumstances surrounding his death remained officially closed.

Prisoner-on-prisoner violence was also a problem. In some cases prison authorities encouraged prisoners to abuse certain inmates. On August 5, four inmates beat a 29-year-old prisoner in Primorskiy Kray, Anton Li. Prison officials brought Li to the hospital only the following day, and he fell into a coma after surgery. There were reports that the inmates carried out the attack under the instruction of prison employees. There were elaborate inmate-enforced caste systems in which certain groups, including informers, gay inmates, rapists, prison rape victims, and child molesters, were considered "untouchables." Prison authorities provided little or no protection to these groups.

Health, nutrition, ventilation, and sanitation standards varied among facilities but generally were poor. Potable water sometimes was rationed. Access to quality medical care remained a significant problem in the penal system.

Tuberculosis and HIV among the country's prison population remained significant problems. The Federal Penitentiary Services reported in 2015 that nearly 4 percent of the country's prison population was infected with tuberculosis, while the HIV rate among prisoners increased 6 percent compared with 2014. No new data were available for 2016. Prosecutor General Chayka stated that more than 62,000 detainees were infected with HIV. In January a local NGO filed a complaint with the prosecutor's office alleging that HIV-positive inmates in St. Petersburg, Murmansk, and Pskov Oblast had not received antiretroviral therapy since May

2015. Prison and healthcare officials acknowledged difficulties procuring the drugs but claimed that the problem was largely resolved. According to a prominent human rights advocate, suppliers were reluctant to sell the necessary drugs to prisons at the low procurement price set by the Ministry of Health. In May an HIV-infected prisoner demanded compensation for not being provided adequate medical treatment. The Ministry of Health did not order sufficient quantities of antiretroviral medicine for inmates in 2015, which, according to Prosecutor General Chayka, posed a serious threat to HIV-infected prisoners' lives. Although all correctional facilities had medical units or health centers, only 41 treatment facilities provided treatment for tuberculosis patients, down from 58 in 2014, and only nine prisons provided medical services for drug addiction.

In a 2012 pilot judgment in the case of *Ananyev v. Russia*, the ECHR noted that inadequate conditions of detention were a recurrent and systemic problem in the country and ordered the government to draft a binding implementation plan to remedy the situation. In 2012 the government submitted an action plan for implementing the court's ruling. Since release of the action plan, however, there have been no significant indications of progress. Prison conditions remained poor, as evidenced by the 44 ECHR judgments issued against the country in 2015 for inhuman and degrading prison conditions.

Administration: Both convicted inmates and inmates in pretrial detention facilities had visitation rights, but authorities could deny access to visitors depending on the circumstances. Authorities allowed prisoners serving a regular sentence four three-day visits with their spouses per year. By law those prisoners with harsher sentences are allowed fewer visitation rights. On occasion prison officials cancelled visits if the prison did not have enough space to accommodate them. The judge in a prisoner's case could deny the prisoner visitation rights. Authorities could also prohibit relatives deemed a security risk from visiting prisoners.

While prisoners could file complaints with public oversight commissions or with the Human Rights Ombudsman's Office, they were often afraid of reprisal. Prison reform activists reported that only prisoners who believed they had no other option risked the consequences of filing a complaint. Complaints that reached the oversight commissions often focused on minor personal requests.

There were no completely independent bodies to investigate credible allegations of inhuman conditions. In 2014 new members were added to public oversight commissions, but appointment and selection procedures prevented many human rights defenders from participating, decreasing the effectiveness of oversight commission observation in many regions. At the same time, authorities increased appointments of former military, police, and prison officials to oversight commissions, effectively placing them under the control of law enforcement agencies. According to activists and media reports, the independence of the oversight commissions varied by region. The newspaper *Vedomosti* reported that, after the selection of new members for the Moscow public oversight commission in 2013, the majority of commission members were former officers of the security services and former prison officials, rather than human rights activists who had historically made up the majority of commission members.

Independent Monitoring: There were no prison ombudsmen. The law regulating public oversight of detention centers allows public oversight commission representatives to visit facilities. According to the Russian Public Chamber, there were public oversight commissions in 81 regions with a total of 1,154 commission members. By law there should be five to 40 members on each commission. Authorities permitted only the oversight commissions to visit prisons regularly to monitor conditions. In October human rights activists expressed concern that several of the most active members of the commissions had been removed and replaced with individuals close to authorities, including many from law enforcement backgrounds. Notably, Dmitriy Komnov, who had overseen the prison where lawyer Sergei Magnitsky died in 2009, was elected to the Moscow public oversight commission. According to the NGO Committee for the Prevention of Torture, public oversight commissions were legally entitled to have access to all prison and detention facilities, including psychiatric facilities, but prison authorities often prevented them from accessing these facilities. The law does not establish procedures for federal authorities to respond to oversight commission findings or recommendations, which are not legally binding.

d. Arbitrary Arrest or Detention

While the law prohibits arbitrary arrest and detention, authorities engaged in arbitrary arrest and detention with impunity.

Role of the Police and Security Apparatus

The Ministry of Internal Affairs, the FSB, the Investigative Committee, the Office of the Prosecutor General, and the National Guard are responsible for law enforcement at all levels of government. The FSB is responsible for security, counterintelligence, and counterterrorism as well as for fighting organized crime and corruption. The national police force under the Ministry of Internal Affairs is organized into federal, regional, and local levels. In April, President Putin established the Russian Federal National Guard Service. This new executive body, which is under the control of the president as the commander in chief, secures borders alongside the Border Guard, administers gun control, combats terrorism and organized crime, protects public order, and guards important state facilities. The National Guard also participates in armed defense of the county's territory together with the Ministry of Defense.

Arrest Procedures and Treatment of Detainees

By law authorities may arrest and hold a suspect for up to 48 hours without court approval, provided there is evidence of the crime or a witness; otherwise, an arrest warrant is required. The law requires judicial approval of arrest warrants, searches, seizures, and detentions. Officials generally honored this requirement, although bribery or political pressure sometimes subverted the process of obtaining judicial warrants. After arrest, police typically take detainees to the nearest police station, where they inform them of their rights. Police must prepare a protocol stating the grounds for the arrest, and both detainee and police officer must sign it within three hours of detention. Police must interrogate detainees within the first 24 hours of detention. Prior to interrogation, a detainee has the right to meet with an attorney for two hours. No later than 12 hours after detention, police must notify the prosecutor. They must also give an opportunity to the detainee to notify his or her relatives by telephone unless a prosecutor issues a warrant to keep the detention secret. Police are required to release a detainee after 48 hours, subject to bail conditions, unless a court decides, at a hearing, to prolong custody in response to a motion filed by police not less than eight hours before the 48-hour detention period expires. The defendant and his or her attorney must be present at the court hearing.

By law police must complete their investigation and transfer a case to a prosecutor for arraignment within two months of a suspect's arrest, although an investigative authority may extend a criminal investigation for up to 12 months. Extensions beyond 12 months need the approval of the head federal investigative authority in the Ministry of Internal Affairs, the FSB, or the Investigative Committee. According to some defense lawyers, the two-month time limit often was exceeded, especially in cases with a high degree of public interest.

A number of problems related to detainees' ability to obtain adequate defense counsel. Federal law provides defendants the right to choose their own lawyers, but investigators generally did not respect this provision, instead designating lawyers friendly to the prosecution. These "pocket" defense attorneys agreed to the interrogation of their clients in their presence while making no effort to defend their clients' legal rights. In many cases, especially in more remote regions, defense counsel was not available for indigent defendants. Judges usually did not suppress confessions of suspects taken without a lawyer present. Judges at times freed suspects held in excess of detention limits, although they usually granted prosecutors' motions to extend detention periods.

Authorities generally respected the legal limitations on detention except in the North Caucasus. There were reports of occasional noncompliance with the 48-hour limit for holding a detainee. At times authorities failed to issue an official detention protocol within the required three hours after detention and held suspects longer than the legal detention limits. The practice was widespread in the North Caucasus (see section 1.g.) and unevenly applied.

Arbitrary Arrest: There were many reports of arbitrary arrest. On February 12 in Dagestan, police detained more than 30 men going to prayer at the local mosque. Witnesses told the independent online news site *Caucasian Knot* that the men were held until evening before being released. None of the men was charged with a crime.

Pretrial Detention: Observers noted that lengthy pretrial detention was a problem, but data on its extent was not available.

Detainee's Ability to Challenge Lawfulness of Detention before a Court: According to the law, a detainee may challenge the lawfulness of detention before an investigator, prosecutor, or court. The challenge can take the legal form of a referral or complaint. The defense typically submits a referral to ask for a certain procedural motion, be it with the prosecution or court, and a complaint is submitted with respect to action that was already taken. Using these instruments, a detainee or his or her lawyer can cause the prosecution or court to change the type of detention used (from arrest in a detention facility to house arrest, for example) or complain that a certain type of pretrial restraint is unlawful. The investigator and the court have absolute discretion to impose limits on the type of detention used if they have sufficient grounds to believe that the defendant will escape from prosecution, continue criminal activity, threaten witnesses or other individuals connected with the criminal case, destroy evidence, or otherwise hamper the investigation.

Statistics related to the number of successful challenges to the lawfulness of detention are not available. The judge typically agrees with the investigator's position and dismisses defense referrals or complaints on this problem.

Protracted Detention of Rejected Asylum Seekers or Stateless Persons: Authorities continued to detain asylum seekers while their cases were pending as well as all rejected asylum seekers prior to deportation or pending judicial review (see section 2.d.). Human rights NGOs reported authorities used protracted detention in such cases, including detention past the legal limit of 12 months.

Amnesty: In May, President Putin pardoned Lieutenant Nadiya Savchenko, a Ukrainian military pilot and Rada deputy, who was released in a prisoner swap in exchange for two Russian intelligence operatives. In March a politically motivated trial had found Savchenko guilty of killing two Russian journalists in Metalist, Ukraine. Putin also pardoned Ukrainian citizens Hennadiy Afanasyev and Yuriy Soloshenko, convicted for "plotting terrorist acts" and espionage, respectively, in a swap in June, this time for two journalists (see section 1.e., Political Prisoners and Detainees).

e. Denial of Fair Public Trial

The law provides for an independent judiciary, but judges remained subject to influence from the executive branch, the armed forces, and other security forces, particularly in high-profile or politically sensitive cases. The outcomes of some trials appeared predetermined.

The human rights ombudsman received 64,189 complaints in 2015, an 18 percent increase over 2014. The largest number of complaints (30 percent) alleged violations of criminal proceedings and violations during trials.

Judges were subject to pressures that could influence the outcome of cases. Former Supreme Court judge Tamara Morshchakova, in an interview on the Moscow Helsinki Group website on August 14, indicated that judges were concerned by how their rulings would be seen by higher courts and often consulted with contacts in the higher courts to make a decision that would not cause them to lose favor or be later overturned. Morshchakova also indicated that the number of individuals instructing judges on rulings was expanding to include local officials, not just superiors.

In many cases authorities reportedly did not provide witnesses and victims adequate protection from intimidation or threats from powerful criminal defendants.

Trial Procedures

The defendant has a legal presumption of innocence. A judge typically hears trials (bench trials). Certain crimes, including terrorism, espionage, hostage taking, and inciting mass disorder, must be heard by panels of three judges. Judges acquitted less than 1 percent of defendants.

The law allows prosecutors to appeal acquittals, which they did in most cases. Prosecutors may also appeal what they regard as lenient sentences. Appellate courts reversed approximately 1 percent of sentences where the defendant had been found guilty and 37 percent where the defendant had been found not guilty and remanded them for a new trial, although these cases often ended in a second acquittal.

During trial the defense is not required to present evidence and is given an opportunity to cross-examine witnesses and call defense witnesses, although judges may deny the defense this opportunity. On March 24, the Jehovah's Witnesses organization in Tyumen appealed to the Russian Supreme Court regarding allegations of extremism against the church, in part because the lower courts refused to allow witnesses for the defense during the trial. Defendants in custody during a trial are confined to a caged area, which was replaced by glass enclosures in some courts. Defendants have the right to be present at the trial and the right to free interpretation as necessary from the moment charged through all appeals. Defendants have the right of appeal. Prior to trial, defendants receive a copy of their indictment, which describes the charges against them in detail. They also have the opportunity to review their criminal file following the completion of the criminal investigation. The law provides for the appointment of an attorney free of charge if a defendant cannot afford one, although the high cost of competent legal service meant that lower-income defendants often lacked competent representation. There were few qualified defense attorneys in remote areas of the country. Defense attorneys may visit their clients in detention, although defense lawyers claimed authorities electronically monitored their conversations and did not always provide them access to their clients. Defendants also have the right not to be compelled to testify or confess guilt.

Plea bargaining was used to settle between 62 and 66 percent of criminal cases in 2015, according to different estimates, and the law allows a defendant to receive a reduced sentence for testifying against others. Plea bargains reduced defendants' time in pretrial detention in approximately 50 percent of cases, reduced the average prison term to no more than half of the otherwise applicable statutory maximum, and allowed courts and prosecutors to devote their resources to other cases.

Political Prisoners and Detainees

There were political prisoners in the country, and authorities detained and prosecuted individuals for political reasons. As of October 31, the Memorial Human Rights Center's updated list of political prisoners included 102 names, more than double the 50 individuals the organization listed in 2015. Those added to the list during the year included Maksim Panfilov, arrested on charges of participation in a mass disturbance and use of nonlethal force against government representatives in connection with the 2012 Bolotnaya Square case. The case concerned clashes between police and protesters at a demonstration on the eve of President Putin's inauguration in 2012. Blogger Aleksey Kungurov, who was accused of public justification of terrorism for his blog pieces criticizing Russian Aerospace Forces' activities in Syria, was also included. In June the *Chronicle of Current Events* published a list of 277 alleged political prisoners that included opposition politicians, human rights activists, environmental activists, religious believers, and bloggers. From this list, approximately one-third were members of the opposition, 40 percent had been prosecuted for religious beliefs, and 8 percent were bloggers or social activists.

On May 5, a blogger from Tver, Andrey Bubeyev, who was found guilty of extremism and calling for separatism, was sentenced to two years in a minimum-security penal colony for having reposted materials on social media against the country's involvement in Ukraine. On March 29, while Bubeyev was being held on remand, the Memorial Human Rights Center recognized him as a political prisoner.

On July 21, the Federal Penitentiary Service filed suit against opposition activist Alexey Navalny, requesting that his suspended sentence be changed to a real prison term in the Yves-Rocher case. On August 1, the Lyublinskiy District Court of Moscow declined to withdraw the suspended sentence. On November 16, the Supreme Court, referencing the European Court of Human Rights' ruling in February that Alexey Navalny's right to a fair trial had been violated, sent the case back to a lower court for review. Aleksey Navalny and his brother Oleg were found guilty of fraud in December 2014 in a case involving the Yves-Rocher company. Aleksey had received a suspended sentence of three and one-half years, while Oleg continued to serve a term of three and one-half years. Observers regarded both cases as politically motivated.

At least one reported political prisoner was held in a psychiatric facility. In July a district court in Chelyabinsk extended the period of mandatory treatment in a psychiatric hospital for Aleksey Moroshkin, a local activist, by six months. Authorities charged Moroshkin with public incitement to separatism via the internet for posting texts in April 2015 calling for the secession of the Ural region from the country. The Memorial Human Rights Center recognized Moroshkin as a political prisoner in July.

Once elected, many opposition politicians reported efforts by the ruling party to undermine their work or remove them from office, often through prosecution (see section 3).

After the country's attempted "annexation" of Crimea in 2014, judicial authorities began in 2015 to transfer court cases to Russia from occupied Crimea for trial. While there were no new notable cases during the year, the son of prominent exiled Crimean Tatar leader Mustafa Jemilev, Khaiser Jemilev, whom Russian authorities in 2014 transferred from the territory of occupied Crimea to Krasnodar Kray, charged with manslaughter, and sentenced in June 2015, was held in Russia until he completed his sentence in November.

On June 14, Putin pardoned Ukrainian citizens Hennadiy Afanasyev and Yuriy Soloshenko in a swap for two journalists held in Ukraine. Afanasyev was a codefendant in the case against Oleh Sentsov. In August 2015 the Northern Caucasus Military District Court sentenced Sentsov, a Ukrainian filmmaker, to 20 years in a prison camp after convicting him on terrorism charges widely seen as politically motivated. The other defendants in the case, Hennadiy Afanasyev, Oleksiy Chirniy, and Oleksandr Kolchenko, received sentences ranging from seven to 10 years. The men were detained in 2014 on suspicion that they were plotting terrorist acts in association with the Right Sector nationalist group. Soloshenko had been sentenced to six years in a penal colony for espionage.

On March 22, Lieutenant Nadiya Savchenko, an Ukrainian military pilot and member of the Ukrainian Parliament (Rada) detained by Russian authorities since 2014, was sentenced to 22 years in prison; the verdict came into force on April 5. On May 25, President Putin pardoned Savchenko, and she was released in a prisoner swap in exchange for two Russian intelligence operatives, Yerofeyev and Aleksandrov, who had been detained in Donbas and sentenced to 14 years in prison. Savchenko returned to Ukraine upon release. Her politically motivated trial on charges of killing two Russian journalists in Metalist, Ukraine, began in Donetsk, Russia, in September 2015. Savchenko also faced charges of attempted murder and entering Russia illegally, even though she was detained in Ukraine and taken to Russia by Russian authorities. She pleaded not guilty to the charges.

On May 26, Ukrainians Mykola Karpyuk and Stanislav Klikh, accused of participating in military activities against Russian armed forces during the conflict in Chechnya in the 1990s, were convicted. Karpyuk was sentenced to 22.5 years' and Klikh to 20 years' imprisonment in a strict regime penitentiary facility.

There were continued court rulings and arrests related to the 2012 Bolotnaya Square case. Many human rights groups considered the Bolotnaya case to have been politically motivated. On April 7, Maksim Panfilov was arrested, becoming the 36th individual accused in the case. On August 29, a Moscow district court extended detention for Panfilov until January 2017. Detention of another Bolotnaya case defendant arrested in December 2015, Dmitriy Buchenkov, was extended until December 2.

There were reports that authorities filed politically motivated charges of treason and espionage against individuals, often in connection with the conflict in Ukraine. The government defines treason to include providing assistance to a foreign state or international organization directed against the country's national security. The Judicial Department under the Russian Supreme Court reported that in 2015, the most recent year for which the data is available, authorities convicted 28 persons on such charges, nearly twice as many as in the previous year. According to the NGO Moscow Public Supervisory Commission, several dozen scientists, entrepreneurs, police officers, and even mothers of small children were convicted of treason in the previous two years on charges classified as "secret" and heard in closed court proceedings.

On July 14, the Moscow City Court sentenced a former employee of the Department of External Church Relations of the Moscow Patriarchate, Evgeniy Petrin, to 12 years in a strict regime prison colony for treason. Petrin, who had been stationed in Kyiv, was arrested in 2014 and has been in custody since. The trial was closed to the public, but according to his lawyer, Petrin was an employee of the FSB and had been gathering information in that capacity. He was convicted of treason for sharing secrets with a foreign country. Petrin claimed innocence and has stated he was tortured to gather evidence against him.

On July 18, the FSB detained in Russia an official translator working for the Organization for Security and Cooperation in Europe (OSCE) special monitoring mission in Ukraine, Artem Shetakov, arresting him as an agent of the Ukrainian security services. He was deported to Ukraine and denied further entry into Russia.

Civil Judicial Procedures and Remedies

Although the law provides mechanisms for individuals to file lawsuits against authorities for violations of civil rights, these mechanisms often did not work well. For example, the law provides that a defendant who has been acquitted after a trial has the right to compensation from the government. While this legal mechanism exists in principle, in practice it was very cumbersome to use. Persons who believed their civil rights had been violated typically sought redress in the ECHR after domestic courts had ruled against them. In 2015 the country passed a law enabling the Constitutional Court to review rulings from international human rights bodies and declare them "nonexecutable" if the court found that the ruling contradicts the constitution. In April the Constitutional Court for the first time declared a ruling by the ECHR, in which the ECHR ruled that the absolute ban on the voting rights of prisoners was in violation of the European Convention on Human Rights, to be nonexecutable under this law.

f. Arbitrary or Unlawful Interference with Privacy, Family, Home, or Correspondence

The law forbids officials from entering a private residence except in cases prescribed by federal law or when authorized by a judicial decision. The law also prohibits the collection, storage, utilization, and dissemination of information about a person's private life without his or her consent. While the law previously prohibited government monitoring of correspondence, telephone conversations, and other means of communication without a warrant, the "Yarovaya package" of amendments to antiterrorism laws came into effect on July 20. These amendments grant authorities sweeping new powers and require telecommunications providers to store all electronic and telecommunication data, including telephone calls, text messages, images, and videos, for six months. Metadata on all communications must be stored for three years and provided to law enforcement authorities upon request. The telecommunications provisions were scheduled to come into effect in

July 2018. There were allegations that government officials and others engaged in electronic surveillance without appropriate authorization and entered residences and other premises without warrants.

Law enforcement agencies require telecommunications service providers to grant the Ministry of Internal Affairs and the FSB continuous remote access to client databases, including telephone and electronic communication and records, enabling police to track private communications and monitor internet activity without the provider's knowledge. The law permits authorities to monitor telephone calls in real time, with a warrant. The Ministry of Information and Communication requires telecommunications service providers to allow the FSB to tap telephones and monitor information over the internet. The Ministry of Information and Communication maintained that authorities would not access information without a court order, although the FSB is not required to show it upon request.

Officials often singled out persons with dark complexions from the Caucasus as well as individuals who appeared to be of African or Asian origin for document checks. There were credible reports that police arbitrarily imposed fines on unregistered persons in excess of legal requirements or demanded bribes.

g. Abuses in Internal Conflict

Violence continued in the North Caucasus republics, driven by separatism, interethnic conflict, jihadist movements, vendettas, criminality, excesses by security forces, and the activity of terrorists. Media reported that in 2015 the total number of deaths and injuries due to the conflicts in the North Caucasus decreased significantly compared with 2014 in all republics of the North Caucasus. According to human rights activists in the region, violence in Dagestan continued at a high level. Dagestan remained the most violent area in the North Caucasus, with approximately 60 percent of all casualties in the region in 2015. Local media described the level of violence in Dagestan as the result of Islamic militant insurgency tactics continuing from the Chechen conflict as well as of the high level of organized crime in the region.

Killings: *Caucasian Knot* reported that in 2015 at least 206 deaths and 49 injuries in the North Caucasus resulted from armed conflicts in the region. With 126 deaths from armed conflict in 2015, Dagestan was the most deadly region. Of the deaths in Dagestan, 97 were militants, 16 were civilians, and 13 were law enforcement officers. This represented a significant decrease from 2014, with the number of casualties in Dagestan down by just over half overall and by nearly 60 percent. The sharpest decrease in violent incidents took place in Chechnya, where the number of deaths decreased to 12 in 2015, compared with 52 in 2014, and the number of injuries fell from 65 to 16.

There continued to be reports that use of indiscriminate force by security forces resulted in numerous deaths or disappearances and that authorities did not prosecute the perpetrators. The Memorial Human Rights Center reported that, on January 1, the body of Khizir Yezhiyev, an economics professor at Grozny State Oil Technical University in Chechnya, was found in the woods near the village of Roshni-Chu in Urus-Martanovskiy district. The medical report stated he died from internal bleeding with six broken ribs, a pierced lung, and many visible injuries on his body. Official reports stated that he died from injuries after falling from a cliff. In December 2015 witnesses claimed to have seen security officials arrest Yezhiyev at a garage in Grozny and take him to an unknown location. According to a number of witnesses, the detainee was taken to one of Grozny's Zavodskiy district police headquarters.

Local militants continued to engage in violent acts against local security forces, often resulting in deaths.

Abductions: Government personnel, militants, and criminal elements continued to engage in abductions in the North Caucasus. According to the prosecutor general, as of 2011 there were more than 2,000 unsolved disappearances in the North Caucasus District. According to data from *Caucasian Knot*, the official list of missing persons in the North Caucasus contained 7,570 names. Local activists asserted that the number of missing persons in Chechnya was much higher than officially reported, potentially up to 20,000 individuals. Amnesty International (AI) reported that law enforcement agencies continued to rely on security operations as the primary method of combating armed groups and continued to be suspected of resorting to enforced disappearances, unlawful detention, as well as torture and other mistreatment of detainees.

There were also accounts of persons being detained by police or unknown individuals. The Memorial Human Rights Center reported that, on April 1, security forces removed from their homes two journalists and authors of "historical" and "linguistic" theories affirming the exceptional nature of the Chechen ethnicity and language, the antiquity of the Chechens, and their status as God's chosen people. On April 5, one of them posted on Facebook that he had not been abducted but was spending four days in the Oktyabrskoye District

Department of Internal Affairs in Grozny, where he was detained to prevent his disappearance; the post was later removed. On April 6, the head of Chechnya, Ramzan Kadyrov, posted on Instagram that the authors had "apologized to the academic community and the clergy of Chechnya" for their writings.

In Chechnya the local Ministry of Public Health continued issuing genetic passports to relatives of individuals who were kidnapped or disappeared during the first and second Chechen conflicts. The genetic passport offers relatives the ability to identify remains that may belong to their family. Between January and July 2015, an estimated 32 Chechen residents received genetic passport, bringing the total to more than 300. Chechnya's Ministry of Internal Affairs claimed to have a database containing 3,016 missing persons, but human rights activists believed the actual number of missing persons to be higher.

<u>Physical Abuse, Punishment, and Torture</u>: Armed forces and police units reportedly abused and tortured both militants and civilians in holding facilities.

The Memorial Human Rights Center reported that in October 2015 police in the Dagestani village of Gotsali detained a 43-year-old man, seizing a hunting rifle with ammunition and planting a bag of marijuana on him. For two days his relatives were unable to locate him. At a hearing three days after his arrest, the man's relatives claimed he had to be carried into the courtroom because he could not walk on his own. Although he was supposed to be released after the hearing, the man was then charged on an administrative offense for speaking abusively and held for an additional three days. After 13 days in custody, the man reported that authorities had taken him with a bag over his head to an undisclosed location, subjected him to electric shocks, and urged him to confess to aiding insurgents.

Human rights groups noted authorities often did not act to address widespread reports of physical abuse of women.

The law requires relatives of terrorists to pay the cost of damages caused by an attack, which human rights advocates criticized as collective punishment. The Memorial Human Rights Center reported that Chechen Republic authorities have upheld the principle of collective responsibility in punishing the relatives of alleged members of illegal armed groups. In 2014 the head of the Chechen, Republic Kadyrov, posted on Instagram, "It shall no longer be said that parents are not responsible for the deeds of their sons and daughters. They will be responsible in Chechnya!" and, "If an insurgent murders a police officer or anyone else in

Chechnya, his family will be immediately thrown out of Chechnya and banned from returning, and their home will be destroyed down to its very foundations."

The Memorial Human Rights Center and *Caucasian Knot* reported that, following an armed attack by two militants on a checkpoint in the village of Alkhan-Kala in Grozny's rural district in May, the homes of the attackers' families were set on fire. Local security officials arrested a journalist who photographed the burnt-out remains of one of the houses, allegedly on suspicion of collusion with Da'esh.

Section 2. Respect for Civil Liberties, Including:

a. Freedom of Speech and Press

While the constitution provides for freedom of speech and press, the government increasingly restricted those rights. The government instituted several new laws that restrict both freedom of speech and press. Regional and local authorities used procedural violations and restrictive or vague legislation to detain, harass, or prosecute persons who criticized the government. The government exercised greater editorial control over state-controlled media than it had previously, creating a media landscape in which most citizens were exposed to predominantly government-approved narratives. Significant government pressure on independent media constrained coverage of numerous problems, especially the situation in Ukraine and Syria, LGBTI problems, the environment, elections, criticism of local or federal leadership, as well as issues of secessionism or federalism. Self-censorship in television and print media was increasingly widespread, particularly on points of view critical of the government or its policies. The government used direct ownership or ownership by large private companies with government links to control or influence major national media and regional media outlets, especially television.

Freedom of Speech and Expression: Government-controlled media frequently used terms such as "traitor," "foreign agent," and "fifth column" to describe individuals expressing views critical of or different from government policy, leading to a climate intolerant of dissent. Authorities also invoked a law prohibiting the "propaganda" of nontraditional sexual relations to minors to restrict the free speech of LGBTI persons and their supporters (see section 6).

Authorities continued to misuse the country's expansive definition of extremism as a tool to stifle dissent. As of November 9, the Ministry of Justice expanded its list of extremist materials to include 3,897 books, videos, websites, social media pages, musical compositions, and other items, an increase of nearly 800 items from 2015. According to the Investigative Committee, detectives referred more than 500 extremism cases to prosecutors in 2015, a number of which included charges of "extremism" levied against individuals for exercising free speech on social media and elsewhere.

In July 2015 journalist Alexander Sokolov of the independent news company RBK was arrested on a charge of participating in the activities of the People's Will Army, which was declared an extremist organization by the Moscow City Court. Sokolov maintained he was simply providing professional services to the group, such as registering its website. Sokolov had previously reported on state corruption and embezzlement connected with the construction of the Vostochnyy space center. In November 2015 the Memorial Human Rights Center recognized Sokolov as a political prisoner, demanding that the court drop its prosecution. In June, Human Rights Ombudswoman Tatyana Moskalkova appealed to the prosecutor general, requesting verification of the lawfulness and legality of the decisions taken in the case against Sokolov. On August 1, Reporters without Borders requested that authorities immediately release Sokolov. He remained in prison.

Several persons, including minors in some instances, were charged with extremism under the criminal code for comments and images posted in online forums. In April, Yekaterina Vologzheninova, a single mother working as a cashier in the central Russian city of Yekaterinburg, was charged after she shared links online critical of the country's role in the Ukraine conflict. She was subsequently sentenced to 320 hours of "corrective labor." According to the indictment, Vologzheninova shared and liked posts deemed "insulting and degrading to Russian people."

By law authorities may close any organization that a court determines to be extremist, including media outlets and websites. Roskomnadzor, Russia's media oversight agency, routinely issued warnings to newspapers and internet sources suspected of publishing extremist materials. Three warnings in one year were enough to initiate a closure lawsuit.

<u>Press and Media Freedoms</u>: The government increasingly restricted press freedom. As of 2015, the latest year for which data was available, the government and state-owned or state-controlled companies directly owned more than 60 percent of the country's 45,000 registered local newspapers and periodicals. The federal or local governments or progovernment individuals completely or partially owned

approximately 66 percent of the 2,500 television stations, including all six national channels. Government-owned media outlets often received preferential benefits, such as rent-free occupancy of government-owned buildings. At many government-owned or controlled outlets, the state increasingly dictated editorial policy. A 2014 law, effective in January, restricts foreign ownership of media outlets to no more than 20 percent.

In May the owner of RBK, Mikhail Prokhorov, who was widely seen as under pressure from the government, fired the chief editors of RBK's newspaper, television channel, and web portal. Following several of RBK's high-profile investigations into corruption on the part of President Putin, his family, and alleged business associates, culminating in reporting on the "Panama Papers" scandal in April, the government allegedly demanded changes in the holding company's editorial policies. The editors in chief were replaced by new personnel from the state-owned TASS news agency. The new editors instructed staff that there would now be a "double line" editorial policy--a line that cannot be crossed--concerning certain types of topics, according to a transcript of an RBK staff meeting published by the newspaper *Meduza* and a source cited in Reuters.

In April the FSB raided the Prokhorov-owned ONEXIM Group's Moscow premises on suspicion of tax evasion. According to a number of analysts, the raids resulted from the government's displeasure with RBK's extended coverage of the Panama Papers leak of documents that detailed how private individuals and public officials used offshore accounts to conceal financial activity, at least some of questionable legality. The Ministry of Internal Affairs also opened a criminal case against RBK on suspicion of alleged fraud.

In July, Svetlana Bababeva, the chief editor of Gazeta.ru, one of the most widely read independent digital media sites in the country, was abruptly fired without explanation when her contract expired. Press reports subsequently indicated that the leadership of Rambler & Co, the media-holding firm that owns Gazeta.ru, faced government pressure to terminate Bababeva because of her opposition to the government and its policies.

Many newspapers ensured their financial viability by agreeing to various types of "support contracts" with government ministries, under which they agreed to provide positive coverage of government officials and policies in news stories. Absent direct government support, independent news publications reported difficulty attracting advertising and securing financial viability, since advertisers feared retaliation if their brands became linked to publications that criticized the government.

<u>Violence and Harassment</u>: Journalists continued to be subjected to arrest, imprisonment, physical attack, harassment, and intimidation as a result of their reporting. The Glasnost Defense Fund reported numerous actions against journalists in 2014, including five killings, 52 attacks, 107 detentions by law enforcement officers, 200 prosecutions, 29 threats against journalists, 15 politically motivated firings, and two attacks on media offices.

On July 12, the Federal Financial Monitoring Service, tasked with monitoring legal entities' and individuals' compliance with the country's terrorist and extremist financing laws, published a list of some 6,000 individuals on its website that included Crimean journalists Nikolay Semena and Anna Andriyevskaya from the Center for Journalistic Investigations. OSCE media freedom representative Dunja Mijatovic expressed concern over the government's placing of journalists on a list of alleged terrorists and extremists.

In September a criminal court in Chechnya's Shali District convicted *Caucasian Knot* journalist Zhalaudi Geriyev of drug possession for personal use and sentenced him to three years in prison. The defense maintained that the prosecutor's case was marred by inconsistencies and flawed evidence as well as by violations of the criminal procedure code. Although Geriyev had signed a confession while in custody, he completely recanted during the trial, claiming he signed the confession under duress. *Caucasian Knot* published a statement stating it believed the criminal case against Geriyev was fabricated and calling accusations of his drug use "completely far-fetched." The statement continued that the "absence of direct evidence" and the pressure placed on Geriyev suggested that the prosecution was "connected with his professional activities."

Journalists reporting in or on the North Caucasus remained particularly vulnerable to physical attacks for their reporting. Rumors also persisted of an alleged "hit list" that included prominent journalists such as Aleksey Venediktov, chief of the independent radio and news organization *Ekho Moskvy*.

There was no progress during the year in establishing accountability in a number of high-profile killings of journalists, including the 2004 killing of Paul Klebnikov, the 2006 killing of Anna Politkovskaya, or the 2009 killing of Natalia Estemirova.

Journalists and bloggers who uncovered various forms of government malfeasance also faced harassment, either in the form of direct threats to their physical safety or threats to their security or livelihood, often through legal prosecution. In March journalists on a reporting tour organized by the Committee for the Prevention of Torture were stopped and beaten by a group of masked assailants as they traveled from Ingushetia to Chechnya. No one was prosecuted for the attack (see section 1.c.).

Censorship or Content Restrictions: The government continued to use laws and decrees to censor or restrict media content.

On January 23, political analyst Andrey Piontkovskiy posted an article to the *Ekho Moskvy* website entitled "A Bomb Ready to Explode" which implied that federal authorities had "lost the war for Chechnya" and suggested federal authorities were complicit in acts of corruption by Chechnya's leaders. The final two paragraphs of the article suggested that authorities allow Chechnya to secede from the Russian Federation and were removed from the text shortly after the article was uploaded. The State Duma called for the prosecution of *Ekho Moskvy* over the article, and the FSB began an investigation of the station for incitement to violate the territorial integrity of the Russian Federation. The FSB conducted searches at *Ekho Moskvy's* editorial office, where they seized Piontkovsky's correspondence. A number of *Ekho Moskvy* employees were also summoned for questioning. A criminal case was opened against Piontkovskiy, who subsequently left the country.

According to the Glasnost Defense Fund and other NGOs, authorities used media's widespread dependence on the government for access to property, printing, and distribution services to discourage critical reporting. Approximately 90 percent of print media relied on state-controlled entities for paper, printing, and distribution services, and many television stations relied on the government for access to the airwaves and office space. Officials continued to manipulate the price of printing at state-controlled publishing houses to pressure private media rivals.

Libel/Slander Laws: Officials at all levels used their authority, sometimes publicly, to restrict the work of journalists and bloggers who criticized them, including taking legal action for alleged slander or libel.

National Security: The law places limits on free expression on national security grounds, notably in statutes against extremism and treason (see Freedom of Speech and Expression).

The government utilized antiextremism laws to censor an array of online content (see Internet Freedom, below).

Internet Freedom

The government took significant new steps to restrict free expression on the internet. Threats to internet freedom included: physical attacks on bloggers; politically motivated prosecutions of bloggers for "extremism," libel, or other crimes; blocking of specific sites by national and local service providers; distributed denial-of-service attacks on sites of opposition groups or independent media, including to independent pollster Levada Center less than two weeks before State Duma elections; monitoring by authorities of all internet communications; and attempts by national, local, and regional authorities to regulate and criminalize content. The internet was widely available to citizens in all parts of the country, although connection speeds varied by region. According to data compiled by the International Telecommunication Union, approximately 73 percent of the country's population used the internet in 2015.

A report issued by the legal services NGO AGORA stated that the number of cases in which authorities infringed the rights of internet users increased in 2015, from 2,951 cases to 15,022. The report attributed the surge in cases in part to improved reporting and noted that the number of requests to block, edit, or remove information also increased significantly. Such types of administrative pressure accounted for 11,800 of the reported cases, and occurred in Russian-occupied Crimea as well as in a number of regions of Russia. The number of regions in Russia in which internet users were subjected to serious pressure increased more than twofold to 30 regions.

New laws place additional restrictions on internet freedom. On June 24, President Putin signed into law amendments to the Federal Law on Information, Information Technologies, and Protection of Information and to the administrative code requiring owners of internet search engines ("news aggregators") with more than one million daily users to be accountable for the truthfulness of "publicly important" information before its dissemination. Authorities can demand that content deemed in violation be removed, and they can also impose heavy fines for noncompliance. Dunja Mijatovic, the OSCE special representative on freedom of the media, raised concerns that the law "could result in governmental interference of online information and introduce self-censorship in private companies." The law's provisions enter into force on January 1, 2017.

In September 2015 the country's data on-shoring law went into effect, requiring domestic and foreign businesses to store citizens' personal data on servers located in the country. Critics expressed concern that the law might have negative commercial effects and provide the government with further access to citizens' private information. On November 17, Roskomnadzor, Russia's communications authority, announced that it would block the U.S.-based professional networking website LinkedIn for failure to comply with the law. LinkedIn was the first social networking site targeted under the new law.

On January 1, the country's "right to be forgotten" law entered into force, allowing individuals in the country to block search engine companies from showing search results that contain information about them. Figures with ties to the regime made several attempts to use the law to stifle reporting about their business and political activities. In June the Kuibyshev district court of St. Petersburg began hearings on claims of St. Petersburg billionaire Evgeniy Prigogine against the Yandex search engine. The applicant sought to remove from search engine results links to the website of the NGO Fund to Fight Corruption that contained reporting on Ministry of Defense contracts awarded to Prigogine's companies. Another target was the Fontanka news site, which covered the entrepreneur's funding of an internet "trolling factory" that posted progovernment comments on a paid basis. By August, out of 11 such claims against Yandex, none had been upheld by the courts. In four instances, decisions were favorable to Yandex, in two the plaintiffs dropped their claims, and in two others, the cases were dismissed without hearing.

In August the public organization Roskomsvoboda filed a lawsuit against Google in the Moscow Arbitration Court to require that pages containing reference materials hosted on the website of the SOVA Center be restored in search engine results. These pages had earlier been removed from search results in accordance with provisions of the "right to be forgotten" law. The deleted pages contained reports on two trials related to incitement of hatred. The plaintiffs' representatives asserted that citizens have the right to know that such crimes were committed, who committed them, and where they were committed and that the decision (to remove the material) infringes on the provision in the constitution providing for free flow of information.

Roskomnadzor maintained a federal blacklist of internet sites and required internet service providers (ISPs) to block access to web pages that the agency deemed offensive or illegal, including information that was already prohibited, such as items on the *Federal List of Extremist Materials*. The law gives the prosecutor general and Roskomnadzor authority to demand that ISPs block websites that promote extremist information or "mass public events that are conducted in violation of appropriate procedures." Roskomsvoboda reported that its registry included more than 25,000 sites as of April and estimated that almost 600,000 sites were blocked within the country. Sites other than those officially blacklisted often ended up themselves blocked when they shares the same internet address as a blocked site.

Cell phone service providers cooperated with government security agencies' surveillance of telephone users. In May political activists Oleg Kozlovskiy and Gregoriy Alburov threatened to sue mobile operator MTS for abetting the hacking of their Telegram accounts, an encrypted messaging service popular among activists for its security features. According to Kozlovskiy and Alburov, on April 29, MTS temporarily disabled text messaging services on their phones, allowing a third party trying to hack their accounts to intercept log-in codes sent via text messaging from Telegram.

On July 7, the State Duma passed the "Yarovaya package" of security-related amendments to the law that require telecommunications providers to provide authorities with "backdoors" around encryption technologies used by apps like WhatsApp, Viber, and Telegram. Providers face fines of one million rubles ($15,000) for noncompliance. Later that month President Putin ordered the FSB to produce encryption keys to decrypt all data on the internet. In the beginning of August, the FSB announced that it finally had the capabilities to collect encryption keys from internet companies that could decrypt unreadable data on the internet. The statement met with skepticism in the professional community; due to the nature of encryption key technology, many considered this not feasible.

During the year authorities blocked or threatened to block some websites and social network pages that either criticized government policy or violated laws on internet content. On May 11, users in occupied Crimea and several Russian regions reported that *Krym.Realii*, the Radio Free Europe/Radio Liberty website dedicated to covering events in occupied Crimea, was no longer accessible. In August, after the government alleged Ukrainian "incursions" into the Crimean peninsula, authorities disconnected internet access in the northern part of Crimea, allegedly for security reasons.

During the year authorities prosecuted individual bloggers for alleged extremist content they published online, including the content of other users' comments on their pages. On August 11, a court refused to grant early release on parole to Darya Polyudova, who was sentenced in December 2015 to two years' imprisonment for inciting separatism and extremist activities. The charges derived from three posts related to Ukraine on her VKontakte page that criticized the government for supporting separatists in eastern Ukraine. In February the Investigative Committee opened a case against the prominent blogger Anton Nosik for inciting hatred and humiliation of human dignity. The charges stemmed from a November 2015 post on Nosik's *LiveJournal* blog, titled "Wipe Syria off the Face of the Earth," in which he compared the Assad regime in Syria to the Nazis. Nosik refused to take down the post, asserting that his words did not constitute extremism. His trial remained underway, and he faced four years in prison if convicted. The newspaper *Kommersant* reported that Luzgin faced criminal prosecution under a highly controversial law signed by President Putin in 2014 that imposes penalties ranging from fines to five years' imprisonment for the "rehabilitation of Nazism."

There were multiple reports that authorities fined libraries, schools, and internet clubs during the year for failing to block content listed on the *Federal List of Extremist Materials* or covered under the law "protecting" children from harmful information. The SOVA Center described 27 cases of sanctions directed at the management of educational facilities for various content filtration-related failures from January to August.

The government continued to employ a "system for operational investigative measures," which requires ISPs to install, at their own expense, a device that routes all customer traffic to an FSB terminal. The system enabled police to track private e-mail communications, identify internet users, and monitor their internet activity.

Academic Freedom and Cultural Events

There were indications that the government took new steps during the year to restrict academic and cultural freedom.

Authorities often censored or shut down cultural events or displays that they considered offensive or that expressed views in opposition to the government and in some cases initiated criminal proceedings against organizers. On June 10, a museum dedicated to the newly controversial subject of American and Soviet cooperation in World War II was closed under pressure from administrators of the government school in which it had been located for 12 years. The museum director stated he was offered a lease that would have allowed him to rent space at the school, but the rent was set at an exorbitant rate because administrators knew he had no way of paying. The director subsequently created a mobile version of the museum to travel to different cities in the country.

Those expressing views of historical events that run counter to officially accepted narratives faced harassment. During an annual student essay competition on 20th century Russian history held by the Memorial Human Rights Center in April, progovernment protesters attacked participants, including students and teachers, throwing eggs and green fast-dye antiseptic liquid at them. The protesters yelled "national traitors" at the participants. Prominent Russian novelist Lyudmila Ulitskaya, who chaired the competition's jury, was among those attacked. Some assailants wore World War II-era uniforms, and the group hoisted a replica Soviet Victory flag and held placards reading, "We don't need alternative history."

b. Freedom of Peaceful Assembly and Association

Freedom of Assembly

The law provides for freedom of assembly, but local authorities increasingly restricted this right. The law requires organizers of public meetings, demonstrations, or marches by more than one person to notify the government, although authorities maintained that protest organizers must receive government permission, not just provide notification. Failure to obtain official permission to hold a protest resulted in the demonstration being viewed as unlawful by law enforcement officials, who routinely dispersed such protests. While numerous public demonstrations took place, on many occasions local officials selectively denied groups permission to assemble or offered alternate venues that were inconveniently or remotely located. The law provides heavy penalties for engaging in unsanctioned protests and other violations of the law on public assembly, up to 300,000 rubles ($4,500) for individuals, 600,000 rubles ($9,000) for organizers, and one million rubles ($15,000) for groups or companies.

Under the law the government may punish "mass rioting," which includes teaching and learning about organization of and participation in "mass riots." The law provides that the government may levy fines for violating protest regulations and rules on holding public events and prohibit nighttime demonstrations and meetings. Protesters who violate the regulations multiple times within a six-month period may be fined up to one million rubles ($15,000) or imprisoned for up to five years. In December 2015 a Moscow court sentenced Ildar Dadin to three years' imprisonment for participation in four protests constituting "repeated violations of the rules on conducting public acts." Two more activists, Irina Kalmykova and 76-

year-old Vladimir Ionov, fled the country to avoid similar charges. In January, Presidential Human Rights Council chairman Mikhail Fedotov criticized the law and called on authorities to remove it from the criminal code.

In April authorities arrested Maxim Panfilov in Astrakhan on charges of taking part in a mass riot and assaulting a police officer, making him the 36th and most recent person charged in connection with the 2012 Bolotnaya Square case. Originally initiated in connection with clashes between police and protesters at demonstrations on the eve of President Putin's inauguration (see section 1.e.), the term for Bolotnaya investigations was extended through September.

There were reports that activists were subject to threats and physical violence in connection with organizing or taking part in public events or protests. In February in Chelyabinsk, unknown attackers beat Vyacheslav Kislitsin, an organizer of a local march to commemorate the killing of opposition leader Boris Nemtsov, outside of the factory where he worked. Kislitsin suffered a heart attack and a broken rib and had to be hospitalized. Kislitsin was quoted as claiming that local police officers were among his attackers.

Police often broke up demonstrations that were not officially sanctioned and at times used disproportionate force when doing so. On April 8, Moscow authorities arrested several protesters, including Dmitriy Boynov, for protesting the construction of a building at Park Dubki. Boynov was beaten by police and hospitalized with a fractured leg as well as contusions on his back and chest (see section 1.c.). On April 29, police in Sochi attacked and dispersed a protest by approximately 100 residents of the Lazarev district against the closure of a pedestrian crossing leading to the sea, according to *Caucasian Knot*. According to witnesses, law enforcement authorities arrived at the peaceful demonstration and began forcibly removing and beating people, leading to the hospitalization of several protesters.

In its annual report in February, AI noted that the right to freedom of peaceful assembly remained severely curtailed. The report also noted that protests were infrequent, their number having declined following severe restrictions introduced in earlier years.

On February 26, the State Duma adopted a law requiring that "motor rallies" and other "tent city" gatherings in public places receive official permission. The new law requires gatherings that will interfere with pedestrian or vehicle traffic to receive official agreement 10 days prior to the event; those that do not affect traffic require three days' notice. Consequently, single-person pickets remained the sole form of public protest that does not require official approval.

Although they do not require official approval, authorities restricted "single-person pickets," which require there be at least 164 feet separating protesters from each other. On June 15, Moscow police arrested opposition leader Leonid Volkov for a single-person picket outside the Federation Council building in Moscow protesting the reappointment of Yuriy Chayka as prosecutor general. According to police, the street where Volkov was protesting was considered "protected territory" and therefore, an illegal venue to stage a picket.

Authorities continued to deprive LGBTI individuals and their supporters of free assembly rights. Despite a Supreme Court ruling that LGBTI individuals are a "protected class" and should be allowed to engage in public activities, the law prohibiting so-called propaganda of homosexuality to minors (see section 6) provides grounds to deny LGBTI activists and their supporters the right of assembly and was used on multiple occasions to interrupt public demonstrations by LGBTI activists. In May, Moscow City officials refused an application by representatives of the LGBTI community to hold a parade, upholding a 2012 decision to prohibit gay parades in Moscow for 100 years, despite an ECHR ruling that the ban contravened the European Convention on Human Rights.

Freedom of Association

The Russian Constitution provides for freedom of association. During the year, however, the government instituted new measures and expanded existing restrictive laws to stigmatize, harass, fine, close, and otherwise raise barriers to membership in organizations that were critical of the government.

Public organizations must register their bylaws and the names of their leaders with the Ministry of Justice. The finances of registered organizations are subject to investigation by tax authorities, and foreign grants must be registered.

The government expanded its use of a 2012 law, which requires NGOs that receive foreign funding and engage in "political activity" to register as foreign agents, to harass, stigmatize, and in some cases halt the operation of NGOs. During the year the Ministry of Justice added 37 NGOs to the list of foreign agents. At the end of the year, 150 NGOs were designated as foreign agents.

In addition to continued widespread inspections of NGOs designated as foreign agents, authorities began to levy heavy fines against NGOs for failing to disclose foreign agent status on websites or printed materials. According to HRW, while authorities inspected a wide range of designated civil society groups from nearly every region of the country, groups that were warned, fined, or prosecuted generally were those active in areas such as election monitoring, human rights advocacy, anticorruption work, and environmental protection. During inspections law enforcement agencies typically brought representatives from as many as a dozen different bodies, including fire inspectors, tax inspectors, and health and safety inspectors, to issue citations to NGOs. In addition, state-controlled media crews frequently accompanied authorities during such inspections. On June 27, authorities also initiated criminal charges for the first time under the foreign agents law against the NGO Union of the Women of the Don. As of August 30, the case was still under consideration.

Organizations the government deemed as foreign agents reported experiencing the social effects of stigmatization, such as being targeted by vandals and online criticism, in addition to losing partners and funding sources and being subjected to smear campaigns in the state-controlled press. As a result some organizations discontinued their work and closed their doors. Notable NGOs that closed included St. Petersburg's Antidiscrimination Center Memorial and the Committee against Torture. In February the Supreme Court of Tatarstan ruled to liquidate the NGO AGORA at the request of the Ministry of Justice for violations of the law on foreign agents. This was the first case of a so-called foreign agent forced to close based on a court ruling.

In May at the behest of President Putin, the government clarified and ultimately expanded the definition of political activities covered under the foreign agent law. Putin signed the related amendments in June. Under the new definition, political activities include: organizing public events, rallies, demonstrations, marches, pickets; organizing and conducting public debates, discussions or presentations; participating in election activities aimed at influencing the result, including election observation and forming commissions; public calls to influence local and state government bodies, including calling for changes to legislation; disseminating opinions and decisions of state bodies by technology; and attempts to shape public political views, including public opinion polls or other sociological research.

On September 5, the Ministry of Justice added the first polling organization, the Levada Center, to the register of foreign agents, for the first time making use of the expanded definition of political activity. The addition came two weeks before the State Duma election and only days after the Levada Center published a poll showing a significant decline in support for the ruling United Russia party. The Levada Center indicated in the press that it would have to close if the decision was not canceled, because conducting polling with such a stigma attached would be impossible. The expanded definition of political activity was widely criticized by civil society NGOs, as well as the government's own Presidential Human Rights Council.

In 2015 the foreign agent law was amended to create a mechanism to allow qualifying NGOs to be removed from the foreign agent list. To be delisted, the NGO in question must submit an application to the Ministry of Justice proving it received no foreign funding or engaged in no political activity within the previous 12 months. If the NGO received any foreign funding, it must have returned the money within three months. The ministry would then initiate an unscheduled inspection of the NGO to determine whether it qualified for removal from the list. During the year only six NGOs were successful in their efforts to qualify for removal from the foreign agent list. In such cases, however, the Ministry of Justice did not remove the organizations from the list on its website but noted in a separate column the date the NGO qualified for removal and "ceased performing the functions of a foreign agent."

Use of the law on "undesirable" foreign organizations expanded during the year with the additions of the National Democratic Institute, the International Republican Institute, and the Media Development Fund to the list of such organizations. The organizations joined the National Endowment for Democracy, Open Society, Open Society Institute Assistance Foundation, and the U.S.-Russia Foundation. According to the definition of the law, a foreign organization may be found undesirable if that group is deemed "dangerous to the foundations of the constitutional order of the Russian Federation, its national security, and defense." To date, authorities have not clarified what specific threats the undesirable NGOs posed to the country. In accordance with the law, any foreign organization deemed undesirable must cease its activities, any money or assets found by authorities may be seized, and any citizens found to be continuing to work with the organization in contravention of the law may face up to seven years in prison.

NGOs engaged in political activities or activities that "pose a threat to the country" that receive support from U.S. citizens or organizations are also subject to suspension under the "Dima Yakovlev" law, which prohibits these NGOs from having dual Russian-U.S. citizen members.

There were multiple reports that civil society activists were beaten or attacked in retaliation for their professional activities and that law enforcement officials did not adequately investigate the incidents. On March 16, a mob of unidentified individuals attacked Igor Kalyapin, head of the Committee for the Prevention of Torture, in Chechnya. No arrests were made in connection with the attack. The attack occurred a week after masked men, armed with baseball bats, attacked a group of foreign and Russian journalists and activists from Kalyapin's organization, setting their bus on fire. No arrests were made in connection with the attack (see section 1.c.).

In multiple cases authorities arbitrarily arrested and prosecuted civil society activists in political retaliation for their work (see sections 1.d. and 1.e.).

There were reports that authorities targeted NGOs and activists representing the LGBTI community for retaliation (see section 6, Acts of Violence, Discrimination, and Other Abuses Based on Sexual Orientation and Gender Identity).

c. Freedom of Religion

See the Department of State's *International Religious Freedom Report* at www.state.gov/religiousfreedomreport/.

d. Freedom of Movement, Internally Displaced Persons, Protection of Refugees, and Stateless Persons

The law provides for freedom of internal movement, foreign travel, emigration, and repatriation. With the exception of refugees from Ukraine, who as a group were well received, the government provided minimal assistance to refugees, asylum seekers, stateless persons, and other persons of concern.

Abuse of Migrants, Refugees, and Stateless Persons: The Office of the UN High Commissioner for Refugees (UNHCR) and NGOs stated that police at times detained, fined, and threatened migrants, refugees, and stateless persons with deportation and that citizens subjected them to racially motivated assaults.

The government seldom cooperated on asylum and refugee problems with UNHCR and other humanitarian organizations.

<u>In-country Movement</u>: Although the law gives citizens the right to choose their place of residence, adult citizens must carry government-issued internal passports while traveling domestically and must register with local authorities after arriving at a new location. Persons with official refugee or asylum status must request permission to relocate to a district other than the one that originally granted them status. Authorities often refused to provide government services to individuals without internal passports or proper registration, and many regional governments continued to restrict this right through residential registration rules that closely resembled Soviet-era regulations.

Authorities required intercity travelers to show their internal passports when buying tickets to travel via air, long-distance railroad, water, or road. Commuter travel on road, water, or via railroad did not require identification. Authorities imposed travel restrictions on individuals facing prosecution for political purposes. In August authorities charged Leonid Volkov, the head of the Democratic Opposition's election movement in Novosibirsk, with obstructing the work of a journalist. Authorities reportedly restricted his freedom to travel while they investigated the case.

<u>Foreign Travel</u>: The law provides for freedom to travel abroad, but the government introduced new restrictions on this right during the year, including an amendment that allows for the temporary restriction of citizens' rights to exit the country if they are bankrupt.

The law on procedures for departing from and entering the country stipulates that a person who violates a court decision has no right to leave the country. A court may prohibit a person from leaving the country for failure to satisfy debts, if the individual is suspected, accused, or convicted of a crime, or if the individual has access to classified material. Authorities imposed travel restrictions on individuals facing prosecution for political purposes.

According to press reports, in 2014 the government restricted foreign travel by approximately five million government employees, mostly from the security services. This included employees of the Prosecutor General's Office, the Ministry of Internal Affairs, the Ministry of Defense, the Federal Prison Service, the Federal Drug Control Service, the Federal Bailiff Service, the Federal Migration Service (FMS, now GAMI, see next paragraph), and the Ministry of Emergency Situations. Freedom House reported that often employees who were not themselves prohibited from travel felt obliged not to go abroad to be consistent with colleagues. The law requires citizens to disclose any dual citizenship.

On April 5, the FMS was abolished, and President Putin announced the Ministry of Internal Affairs would take over all FMS duties. The move was part of the larger restructuring of the ministry, which included the creation of the new Russian Federal National Guard Service (see section 1.d, Role of the Police and Security Apparatus). The new entity carrying out the FMS's previous duties is the General Administration for Migration Issues (GAMI). The transfer of responsibility was underway during the year, although officially the FMS ceased operations in April.

Exile: There were many high-profile cases of self-imposed exile during the year, primarily involving leaders of political opposition movements, NGOs, environmental organizations, and protesters who feared reprisals for their participation in anti-Putin demonstrations or for their opposition activities.

Internally Displaced Persons

In December 2014 the Internal Displacement Monitoring Center estimated that Russia was home to at least 27,000 internally displaced persons (IDPs), most of whom remained in the North Caucasus as a result of the Chechen conflict. The situation for the IDPs displaced after the conflict in Chechnya remained poor, with the majority still living in substandard accommodations without proper sanitation and electricity. The government's official statistics showed the number IDPs decreased from 28,292 in 2015 to 25,359 during the year.

Protection of Refugees

Access to Asylum: The country's laws provide for the granting of asylum or refugee status, and the government has established a system for providing protection to refugees. NGOs reported applicants commonly paid informal "facilitation fees" of approximately 33,000 rubles ($500) to GAMI/the FMS adjudicators to have their application reviewed. Applicants who did not speak Russian had to pay for a private interpreter. Human rights organizations noted that nearly all newly arrived refugees and temporary asylum seekers in large cities, in particular Moscow and St. Petersburg, were forced to apply in other regions, allegedly due to full quotas. With the exception of Ukrainians, GAMI/the FMS approved a small percentage of applications for refugee status and temporary asylum.

Some observers pointed out that GAMI/the FMS data failed to include asylum seekers who were forcibly deported or extradited before exhausting their legal remedies. Some asylum seekers, especially those from Central Asia, also reportedly chose not to make formal applications for asylum because doing so often led to criminal investigations and other unwanted attention from the security services.

Human rights organizations criticized the country's reported preferential treatment of Ukrainian applicants for refugee status and temporary asylum. According to UNHCR and local NGOs, authorities had blanket authority to grant temporary asylum to Ukrainians and prioritized Ukrainian nationals over other nationalities, especially those from African nations. As of November 2015, the vast majority of Ukrainian nationals who applied for temporary asylum received this status on a one-year basis and were eligible to apply twice for renewals. This prioritization resulted in longer waiting periods and drastically fewer approvals for non-Ukrainian applicants. As of November 2015, authorities reportedly also had blanket authority to grant temporary asylum to Syrians. According to local NGOs, GAMI/the FMS stopped granting them temporary asylum and refugee status. Local migration experts noted a decrease in the number of Syrians with temporary asylum, indicating that GAMI/the FMS did not renew the temporary asylum of hundreds of Syrians. Authorities did not release up-to-date data on non-Ukrainian refugees during the year. According to official statistics, there were 311,134 Ukrainian citizens holding temporary asylum; in contrast, 1,302 Syrians held the same status.

According to official statistics, 770 persons were granted refugee status during the year, down from 790 in 2015 but more than the 632 reported in 2014.

According to a Sky News report from May, only two Syrians received full asylum status since the conflict there began in 2011. The country's official statistics indicated that two Syrians per year were granted refugee status since 2013. The Sky News report stated that five Syrian asylum seekers in Makhachkala, Dagestan, who had been behind bars for over a year, remained incarcerated indefinitely due to a lack of proper paperwork related to their asylum claims. Human rights groups believed numerous Syrians sat in similar circumstances throughout the country.

In the fall of 2015, approximately 5,500 migrants and asylum seekers crossed Russia's border with Norway by utilizing a loophole that allowed border crossing via bicycle without documentation check by Russian border guards. When Norway began returning the migrants to Russia, HRW noted "a lack of assurance from the Russian authorities that they would provide those sent back with any hearing of their asylum claims, much less a fair consideration of their applications." According to HRW, UNHCR and Norway's country-of-origin office noted deficiencies in Russia's asylum system that could prevent the fair and effective assessment of a person's refugee claims.

Refoulement: The government provided some protection against the expulsion or return of persons to countries where their lives or freedom would be threatened on account of their race, religion, nationality, membership in a particular social group, or political opinion. The responsible agency, GAMI/the FMS, did not maintain a presence at airports or other border points and did not adequately publicize that asylum seekers had the ability to request access to the agency. Asylum seekers had to rely on the goodwill of border guards and airline personnel to call immigration officials. Otherwise, they faced immediate return to their countries of origin, including in some cases to countries where they may have had reasonable grounds to fear persecution.

A Sky News report stated that Russian officials had tried to deport five detained asylum seekers directly back to Syria, but their attorney succeeded in blocking the deportation while they were waiting to board a plane at a Moscow airport. According to UNHCR and other human rights monitors, at least 18 Syrians have been directly returned to Syria, contravening the country's constitution.

By law an applicant may appeal the decision of a GAMI/the FMS official to a higher-ranking authority or to a court. During the appeal process, the applicant is legally entitled to the rights of a person whose application for refugee status was being considered.

Human rights groups continued to allege that authorities made improper use of international agreements that permit them to detain, and possibly repatriate, persons with outstanding arrest warrants from other former Soviet states. This system, enforced by informal ties between senior law enforcement officials of the countries concerned, permitted authorities to detain individuals for up to one month while the Prosecutor General's Office investigated the nature of the warrants. UNHCR and human rights groups noted several cases of disappearances and extralegal return of persons of UNHCR concern, in which officials detained individuals (most commonly from Central Asia) and returned them to their country of origin clandestinely. Rights groups and UNHCR maintained that this could not have happened without the cooperation of several different federal agencies.

In July, Khursheddin Fazylov, a citizen of Tajikistan who had applied for political asylum in Russia, was returned to Tajikistan before his application and appeals process had been completed. The government of Tajikistan accused him of recruiting Tajik citizens to go to Syria through Turkey to take part in jihad and requested his extradition. According to his lawyer, Fazylov was transported out of the country to Tajikistan on the day his detention period would have expired. At the time, his asylum case was still under appeal. Fazylov's family reported that, within a week of that date, he was back in Tajikistan in prison.

In July the government returned Olim Ochilov, a 27-year-old citizen of Uzbekistan, to his home country, where he allegedly faced the threat of torture. The deportation took place even though the ECHR had ruled that Russia should grant Ochilov temporary asylum. The government of Uzbekistan accused Ochilov of "antistate activities." His location in Uzbekistan was unknown.

Access to Basic Services: By law successful temporary asylum seekers and persons whose applications were being processed have the right to work, receive medical care, and attend school. NGOs reported authorities provided some services to Ukrainian asylum seekers, but applicants from other countries were routinely denied them. During the year authorities closed the majority of government-funded temporary accommodation centers specially erected for Ukrainian nationals waiting to receive temporary asylum. These centers provided shelter, food, medical care, and job-placement assistance. As of November 2015, some 16,112 Ukrainian nationals remained in these centers throughout the country, although NGOs reported that many inhabitants were Ukrainians with legal status who were paying to live in the facilities. Non-Ukrainian asylum applicants did not have access to these benefits.

While federal law provides for education for all children, regional authorities occasionally denied access to schools to children of temporary asylum and refugee applicants who lacked residential registration. When parents encountered difficulties enrolling their children in school, authorities generally cooperated with UNHCR to resolve the problem. Authorities frequently denied applicants the right to work if they lacked residential registration, which was common due to landlords' preference not to register occupants for tax reasons.

Temporary Protection: A person who did not satisfy the criteria for refugee status, but who could not be expelled or deported for humanitarian reasons could receive temporary asylum after submitting a separate application. There were reports, however, of authorities not upholding the principle of temporary protection.

Stateless Persons

UNHCR estimated there were approximately 113,470 stateless persons in the country at the end of 2014. Official statistics did not differentiate between stateless person and other categories of persons seeking assistance. UNHCR reported a significant number of Afghans resided in Russia for more than 20 years, including some orphans brought back by Soviet armed forces. The majority of these individuals and their offspring did not have legal status in the country because GAMI/the FMS repeatedly rejected their applications for temporary asylum or refugee status. This Afghan population faced the same risks as newly arrived asylum seekers, including denial of, or lack of, access to medical care, schooling, and housing.

Section 3. Freedom to Participate in the Political Process

While the law provides citizens the ability to choose their government in free and fair periodic elections held by secret ballot and based on universal and equal suffrage, citizens could not fully do so because the government limited the ability of opposition parties to organize, register candidates for public office, access media, and conduct political campaigns.

The law allows regional authorities to abolish direct mayoral elections in major cities. Only nine of 83 regional capitals retained direct mayoral elections, although two previously elected mayors were still completing their terms. The law does not apply to Moscow and St. Petersburg, since the mayors of these cities have the status of governors.

After allegations of voter fraud in the 2011 State Duma elections sparked mass protests in Moscow and St. Petersburg, authorities sought to curtail the work of independent monitors and promote government-sponsored monitoring. The State Duma passed legislation in February allowing each party or candidate to have up to two election monitors present at each polling station, affirming the right of observers to use photography and video equipment, and banning the removal of observers without a court order. The legislation prohibited observers from being accredited to more than one polling station, sharply limiting the ability of civil society to monitor elections. Critics contended that the legislation makes it difficult for domestic election monitors to conduct surprise inspections due to provisions requiring observers to register with authorities, including the polling station they intend to monitor, three days before elections. The legislation also increased the registration requirements for journalists wishing to monitor elections.

Such regulations hampered the work of independent or nonparty affiliated groups, whose monitors registered as journalists for their affiliated publications. The independent election-monitoring organization Golos reported that the number of independent observers decreased by half since 2011.

Authorities also continued to hamper the efforts of independent monitor Golos, whose work was curtailed by a law that bans organizations listed as foreign agents from taking part in the election process. Critics asserted that the law violates the constitution. In July a Moscow Court liquidated the Defense of Voters' Rights branch of the organization for violations of the foreign agent law. In May a Samara court ruled that the director of Golos-Ural, Lyudmila Kuzmina, was personally liable for the organization's alleged failure to pay taxes on money it received from a foreign official development agency. Critics called the decision politically motivated, noting that the money was received before the foreign agent law went into effect. Golos had nonetheless already paid taxes on the donation, and the law does not provide a basis to hold Kuzmina personally liable.

Central Election Commission (CEC) chairperson Ella Pamfilova publicly stated that, because the federal budget did not provide for video cameras in polling stations, regions wishing such monitoring would have to provide for it from their budgets. Video monitoring of polling stations was cut in 2015. Observer groups insisted authorities eliminated these devices to prevent detection of fraud. In 2015 the CEC announced that bloggers whose web pages received more than 3,000 daily visits could comment on elections only during the officially determined campaign period and post only "objective and verifiable information about candidates and parties that does not infringe on candidates' equality."

Elections and Political Participation

<u>Recent Elections</u>: On September 18, the country held elections to its national legislature, the State Duma. The election marked a return to a mixed election system in which voters elect one-half of the Duma's 450 seats through party list and one-half by candidates representing geographic districts, so-called "single mandate candidates." Elections were held concurrently to select nine governors and/or regional heads and 39 regional legislatures, as well as other local officials. The elections proceeded with fewer allegations of election-day voter fraud than the previous national legislative election in 2011, but the OSCE's Office for Democratic Institutions and Human Rights (ODIHR) observer mission noted that the electoral environment was negatively affected by restrictions to fundamental

freedoms and political rights, firmly controlled media, and a tightening grip on civil society.

The OSCE/ODHIR election observation mission concluded that the liberalization of the party registration process has yet to result in distinct political alternatives. Party registration at the national level, where it was governed by the CEC, tended to proceed more smoothly and inclusively than at the regional level. The CEC endorsed the eligibility of 14 of 22 political parties to register their candidates. The press reported that on average only seven parties were eligible to compete in most regional legislative elections. For example, the Communists of Russia and the Rodina party were unable to register in 16 and 14 regions, respectively. Observers noted that independent candidates and those representing smaller "nonsystemic" parties faced greater hurdles than their counterparts from parties represented in the State Duma. The CEC took a more active role in overturning regional election commissions' unwarranted exclusions of opposition parties. For example, in August the CEC reviewed and overturned the decision of the St. Petersburg election commission to exclude candidates from the opposition party PARNAS, finding "no objective reasons to exclude the party's registration" for elections to the regional legislature. The CEC also restored the opposition Yabloko Party's right to run in the Novgorod regional elections on August 12 and expressed a lack confidence in the regional election commission's chairman, suggesting he should resign.

In other regions problems with the registration of parties remained unaddressed. For example, the Petrozavodsk City Court disqualified Yabloko party's city council slate on August 30. The Karelia Supreme Court upheld the lower court's decision September 12.

During the pre-election period, the government employed tactics to prevent a fair campaign environment, such as the improper use of administrative resources, denying applications for opposition rallies, controlling opposition candidates' mass media coverage, and distributing gifts to potential voters to promote the victory of government-backed candidates in several regions. For example, in a single-mandate district in Orel, the ruling-party candidate and director of a district medical clinic organized a health fair at which free health tests would be provided for the local population. Election activists highlighted that electoral campaign offices were often established within local government offices in violation of election law, but noted that such offices were quickly closed once official complaints were made to local prosecutors.

While the OSCE/ODIHR election observation mission noted that election day generally proceeded in an orderly manner, it cited numerous procedural irregularities, particularly during the counting process. Observers assessed the counting process to be "bad or very bad" in 23 percent of the observed polling stations. The citizen-organized organization Golos, which conducted long- and short-term observation in 40 regions, received 1,798 reports of alleged election-day violations, the most common of which included violations during absentee or "at home" voting, violations of the rights of observers, illegal campaigning, improper tabulation of results, coercion of voters, and breeches of secrecy of the vote. For example, the organization received complaints from 70 polling stations in the Moscow region concerning the practice of mass voting using absentee ballots. Observers gave numerous examples of buses transporting large groups of voters with absentee ballots. In the pre-election campaign, voters allegedly complained that their employers pressured them to obtain such absentee ballots. There were also a number of reports concerning ballot stuffing across the country, sometimes captured on live video by observers. The CEC responded by announcing that a criminal investigation would be initiated against at least one election official in Rostov and cancelling the results of one single-mandate district in Nizhny Novgorod.

Independent organizations and opposition figures faced harassment. For example, St. Petersburg police detained Open Russia party coordinator Vladimir Kara-Murza and Duma candidate Andrey Pivovarov of PARNAS during a meeting with voters on August 24, despite receiving permission from local authorities to meet with voters. In the Republic of Mary El, opposition candidates appealed to the CEC to suspend voting in one single-mandate Duma district in connection with "massive legal violations," including physical and economic threats to supporters of one independent candidate and attempts to intimidate the candidate himself. In response, a representative from the CEC visited the area and ordered an investigation of the complaints.

The OSCE/ODIHR election-monitoring mission noted that representatives of citizen observer groups, such as Golos, Citizen Observer, SONAR, and others registered as media or party observers to monitor elections. The mission concluded that Golos had to operate under unconducive conditions, particularly after it was dissolved as an organization. Golos reported that the number of observers expelled from polling stations dramatically decreased in comparison with elections in 2011.

Opposition candidates had difficulty gaining access to traditional media. For example, Russian press reported that opposition candidates from several parties complained of difficulties concluding contracts with billboard companies in the Moscow region, citing interference from the Moscow governor's office. Many opposition candidates relied on Facebook, Twitter, and VKontakte to connect with voters, since the state-controlled print and television media did not cover their campaigns.

Political Parties and Political Participation: The law requires political parties to have 500 members to register. Some 74 parties successfully completed registration requirements and obtained the right to run in elections.

While parties represented in the State Duma may nominate a presidential candidate without having to collect and submit signatures, prospective presidential candidates from parties without Duma representation must collect two million signatures from supporters throughout the country and submit the signatures to the CEC for certification. An independent candidate is ineligible to run if the commission finds more than 5 percent of the signatures to be invalid.

The law requires gubernatorial candidates not nominated by a registered political party to meet the "municipal filter" requirement. Such signatures of support must be collected in no fewer than 75 percent of municipal councils. Gubernatorial candidates nominated by registered political parties are not required to collect signatures from members of the public, although self-nominated candidates are.

The law establishes a mixed electoral system in which half of the Duma deputies are elected in single-mandate constituencies and half are elected from party lists. The law also sets filters that prevent many small, legally registered parties from competing for party-list seats. Parties are exempt from collecting signatures to participate in elections if they have representation in the sitting Duma, received at least 3 percent of the national vote in the previous Duma election, or were represented in at least one regional legislature. The CEC has registered 14 of the 74 registered political parties, but only 22 submitted their lists to the CEC for approval for the Duma elections under these rules. All other parties that wish to compete for party-list seats in the Duma must gather at least 200,000 signatures from voters, with no more than 7,000 signatures from any one region. Smaller parties could participate in single constituencies even if they were not from a registered political party, provided they collected at least 3 percent of the signatures of voters registered in their districts or at least 3,000 signatures, whichever number is higher.

The law prohibits negative campaigning and provides criteria for removing candidates from the ballot, including for vaguely defined "extremist" behavior. The executive branch and the prosecutor general have broad powers to regulate, investigate, and disqualify political parties. Other provisions limit campaign spending, set specific campaign periods, and provide for restrictions on campaign materials.

Once elected, many opposition politicians reported efforts by the ruling party to undermine their work or remove them from office. In June officials arrested independent Kirov governor Nikita Belykh on corruption charges, and President Putin dismissed him from office several weeks later. Before his 2009 appointment, Belykh served as leader of opposition party Union of Right Forces (see also section 4). In August the former mayor of Yaroslavl, Yevgeniy Urlashov, a member of the opposition whom authorities arrested in 2013 on charges of embezzlement, was found guilty and sentenced to 15 years in a penal colony.

Leaders and members of opposition parties faced prosecution or other forms of retaliation. National and local authorities continued to charge opposition candidates with serious crimes that would prevent them from participating in elections. In April authorities allegedly found Nazi propaganda in the campaign office of local opposition candidate Yegor Savin, who claimed investigators planted the materials. A ban on distributing Nazi propaganda is the only administrative offense that carries a ban on participating in elections.

Participation of Women and Minorities: No laws limit the participation of women and members of minorities in the political process, and women and minorities did participate. Information on the ethnic composition of the State Duma and the Federation Council was not available. While members of national minorities took an active part in political life, ethnic Russians, who constituted approximately 80 percent of the population, dominated the political and administrative system, particularly at the federal level.

Section 4. Official Corruption and Lack of Transparency in Government

The law provides criminal penalties for official corruption, but the government acknowledged difficulty enforcing the law effectively, and officials often engaged in corrupt practices with impunity. The *Global Competitiveness Report 2014-15* compiled by the World Economic Forum cited corruption as the most problematic, high-risk factor for doing business in the country. In March 2015 the government passed a law reducing the ceiling on fines for receiving a bribe (from 25 times the bribe's amount down to 10 times) and for providing a bribe (from 15 times the bribe's amount down to five times).

Corruption was widespread throughout the executive branch, including within the security sector and migration management agencies, as well as in the legislative and judicial branches at all levels of government. Its manifestations included bribery of officials, misuse of budgetary resources, theft of government property, kickbacks in the procurement process, extortion, and improper use of official position to secure personal profits. While there were prosecutions for bribery, a general lack of enforcement remained a problem. Official corruption continued to be rampant in numerous areas, including education, military conscription, health care, commerce, housing, social welfare, law enforcement, and the judicial system. According to the Moscow Police, the average bribe for all purposes during 2015 was approximately 654,000 rubles ($9,810), more than double the amount of the previous year. According to a September 2015 report in the newspaper *Izvestiya*, corruption increased 6.5 percent during the year, with an especially heavy concentration of cases in Pskov, the Jewish Autonomous Oblast, Chelyabinsk, Mordovia, and Bashkortostan.

Corruption: Prosecutors charged high-level officials, including a regional governor, a regional head for economic security and anticorruption for the Ministry of Internal Affairs, a regional Customs Service chief, and a deputy minister of culture with corruption during the year.

In September investigators discovered $123 million in cash in an apartment owned by the sister of Internal Affairs Ministry colonel Dmitriy Zakharchenko, the acting head of one of the ministry's anticorruption units. Zakharchenko was charged with accepting bribes and abuse of authority. In November his pretrial detention was extended through March 8, and the investigation remained underway.

The areas of government spending that ranked highest in corruption were public procurement, media, national defense, and public utilities. The federal Investigative Committee estimated annual damages of 40 billion rubles ($600 million) caused by corruption, although independent estimates put the figure much higher. On April 27, the Prosecutor General's Office reported that more than 32,000 corruption cases were registered in 2015. Of these cases, 13,000 (40 percent) resulted in guilty verdicts. A study by the Prosecutor General's Office found that corruption-related crime in military procurement had increased by 10 percent. In July 2015 the Prosecutor General's Office reported that 7.5 billion rubles ($112 million) had been stolen during construction of the Far East Cosmodrome.

During the year the government adopted legislation imposing criminal penalties for "small commercial bribery" (bribery not exceeding 10,000 rubles or $150) and for "mediation in commercial bribery."

Financial Disclosure: The law prohibits state officials and heads of state-owned enterprises from owning financial assets or bank accounts abroad. The law also requires politicians to file extensive declarations of all foreign real estate they own and civil servants to declare any large expenditure involving land, vehicles, and securities, as well as their incomes. The law was unevenly enforced, and investigative bodies rarely acted upon media reports of undeclared assets held overseas and other alleged violations.

The law requires government officials to submit financial statements, restricts their employment at entities where they had prior connections, and requires reporting of actual or possible corrupt activity. The information that officials provided often did not reflect their true income or that of close family members.

Public Access to Information: The law authorizes public access to government information unless it is confidential or classified as a state secret. The law requires placement of information regarding activities of federal executive agencies on the internet. According to the watchdog website Infometer, government agencies frequently failed to implement the law. Federal agencies published only 40 percent of the information required on the internet, while regional governments published approximately 50 percent. Courts, despite the presumption favoring access, denied citizens' requests for information on the grounds that the data requested did not directly affect their interests.

In June the government released its *National Anticorruption Plan for 2016-2017*.

Section 5. Governmental Attitude Regarding International and Nongovernmental Investigation of Alleged Violations of Human Rights

Domestic and international human rights groups operated in the country, investigating and publicly commenting on human rights problems. Official harassment of independent NGOs continued and in many instances intensified, particularly of groups that focused on election monitoring, exposing corruption, and addressing human rights abuses. NGO activities and international humanitarian assistance in the North Caucasus were severely restricted. Some officials, including the ombudsman for human rights, regional ombudsman representatives, and the chair of the Presidential Human Rights Council, Mikhail Fedotov, regularly interacted and cooperated with NGOs. Fedotov was critical of revisions to the foreign agent law, the expansion of the undesirable foreign organization law, and the introduction of the antiterrorism amendments known collectively as the "Yarovaya package" (see section 2.b.).

The law regulating NGOs requires them to register with the Ministry of Justice. Authorities required NGOs to submit annual reports to the government that disclose sources of foreign funding and detailed information on how they used their funds. By law the Ministry of Justice can register NGOs that receive foreign funding and engage in "political activity" as foreign agents, a stigmatizing term that connotes treason or espionage. NGOs that engaged in political activities, activities that "pose a threat to the country," or activities that receive support from U.S. persons or organizations, are subject to suspension under the "Dima Yakovlev" law. The same law prohibits these NGOs from having dual-U.S. citizen members.

The government used the law on foreign agents to justify unannounced inspections of NGOs; levy fines for noncompliance, liquidation, and prosecution; and demand that they self-register as a foreign agent or be added to the register unilaterally by the Ministry of Justice. By year's end the Ministry of Justice had listed 150 NGOs as foreign agents (see section 2.b.).

The Ministry of Justice pursued efforts intended to discredit or curtail the activities of organizations and foreign agents. The Ministry of Justice attempted to force the closure of several NGOs, including AGORA, an NGO ordered liquidated by the Supreme Court of Tatarstan in the first case of a so-called foreign agent being forced to close based on a court ruling (see section 2.b, Freedom of Association). Several other NGOs, including St. Petersburg's Antidiscrimination Center Memorial, were forced to close due to government harassment, hefty fines, and lack of funding. Golos continued to face severe repression in the form of fines, court hearings, and media harassment by state-owned or controlled media outlets.

High-ranking officials often displayed a hostile attitude towards the activities of human rights organizations and suggested that their work was unpatriotic and detrimental to national security. Konstantin Kosachev, chairman of the Federation Council Committee on International Affairs and author of the council's Patriotic Stop List, told media in April that additional organizations were under consideration for inclusion on the undesirable list. Kosachev, who created the Patriotic Stop List as recommendations to the Prosecutor General's Office of NGOs for inclusion as undesirables, and fellow Federation Council member Andrey Klishas continued to call for the expansion of the undesirable list to counter threats to the country's constitutional order.

Ramzan Kadyrov, the head of the Republic of Chechnya, frequently disparaged and threatened human rights activists and opposition leaders. In February, Kadyrov posted on Instagram an image of PARNAS leader Mikhail Kasyanov and party member Vladimir Kara-Murza in the crosshairs of a gun with a message leading many human rights activists to decry the incident as a threat to murder. In January, Kadyrov called members of the opposition "enemies of the people" who should face trial for sabotage, prompting then human rights ombudswoman Ella Pamfilova to call Kadyrov's statement "harmful." Kadyrov was not charged or reprimanded for either incident.

In March the head of the Committee against Torture, Igor Kalyapin, was attacked when he visited the Chechen capital, Grozny. Local authorities investigated the attack but never filed charges (see section 1.c.). Officials from the Presidential Human Rights Council cancelled a fact-finding trip to Chechnya in June when Kadyrov publicly stated that he could not guarantee the group's safety if Kalyapin would be traveling with them as was planned.

On multiple occasions, President Putin warned the FSB against the "destructive purposes" of NGOs. The terms "foreign agent," "political agent," and "fifth column" were used in official speeches and publications to stigmatize NGOs, opposition politicians, and human rights activists. Putin told the Federal Assembly that presidential grants would be expanded to support "unblemished NGOs."

Authorities continued to apply a number of indirect tactics to suppress or close domestic NGOs, including the application of various laws and harassment in the form of investigations, fines, and raids. They also employed laws on extremism and libel to restrict the activities of NGOs and criticism of the government (see sections 2.a. and 2.b.). Authorities generally refused to cooperate with NGOs that were critical of their activities or listed as a foreign agent. International human rights NGOs had almost no presence east of the Urals. A few local NGOs addressed human rights problems in these regions but often chose not to work on politically sensitive topics to avoid retaliation by local authorities.

Authorities made government funds available to support human rights NGOs to discourage access to foreign support. According to federal budget figures, the government allocated 4.6 billion rubles ($69 million) for NGO grants. A report in the *Moscow Times* published findings that the Russian Orthodox Church was the primary beneficiary of presidential grants the past several years. Many NGOs on the foreign agent list noted that they no longer received funding from the government as a result of the label, particularly NGOs that continued to accept foreign grants.

During the year the government took steps that limited the ability of international organizations to address human rights concerns. On April 19, the Constitutional Court ruled that the country was not obligated to implement a decision by the ECHR regarding prisoners' voting rights, since it contradicted the country's constitution. The case marked the first time that authorities employed a 2015 law granting the government the right to refer ECHR decisions, as well as decisions by other international human rights bodies, to the Constitutional Court for review. According to the law, if a decision by the ECHR or other international body is found to contradict the constitution, the Constitutional Court can reject it.

On November 2, AI staff reportedly arrived at their Moscow office to find the locks had been changed, official seals placed over the doors, and the electricity cut off. City authorities claimed that AI had failed to pay its rent on time, but staff denied that this was the case. On November 3, Fedotov, head of the Russian Human Rights Council, met President Putin and discussed the matter. On November 18, AI signed a new lease agreement with the Moscow property department, after which the staff were allowed to return to the office. The day before the office's closure, AI--a regular critic of the government--had issued a statement calling for the release of imprisoned activist Ildar Dadin and an investigation into his allegations of torture. On December 1, Gazprom-owned television channel NTV aired a report titled "The Amnesty of Terror" on AI, accusing the organization of supporting terrorists and failing to pay rent for its Moscow office. The program further charged that the U.S. Department of State and the CIA sponsored such efforts through charitable organizations such as the Soros Foundation, adding that this is the reason for AI's "high salaries."

On March 12, media reported that the government decided to close the Moscow office of the UN's Office of the High Commissioner for Human Rights (OHCHR). Authorities later confirmed the decision to close the OHCHR office because it had "fulfilled its mission to establish human rights norms in Russia."

<u>Government Human Rights Bodies</u>: Some government institutions continued to promote human rights and intervened in selected abuse complaints, despite widespread doubt as to their effectiveness.

Many observers did not consider the 126-member Public Chamber, composed of appointed members from civil society organizations, to be an effective check on the government. Some prominent human rights groups declined to participate in the chamber due to concern that the government would use it to increase control over civil society.

The Presidential Council for Civil Society and Human Rights is an advisory body to the president tasked with monitoring systemic problems in legislation, keeping track of individual human rights cases, developing proposals to submit to the president and government departments, and monitoring their implementation. Membership in the council increased at the end of 2012 from 40 to 65 members, with the president selecting the new members by decree. Human rights advocates expressed concern that the additions were made to increase progovernment membership and weaken the council's independence.

Human Rights Ombudsman Ella Pamfilova resigned her position to assume a new appointment as head of the Central Elections Commission. In April the Duma elected Tatyana Moskalkova, a Duma deputy and major general in the Ministry of Internal Affairs, to replace Pamfilova as the new commissioner for human rights. The selection of Moskalkova was widely criticized by human rights activists after her statement to the Duma that "human rights issues have been actively used by Western and American bodies as a weapon of blackmail, speculations, threats, attempts to destabilize and exert pressure on Russia."

In March the Ombudsman's Office released its second report from Pamfilova's tenure in the position on the state of human rights in the country. The 252-page report doubled in size from the previous year's report and included input from human rights NGOs, although it was noted in the report that the ombudsman did not necessarily agree with their assessments. The report primarily focused on problems of social inequality, cases of selective justice, a deficit of trust and lack of communication between the authorities at various levels and the general public, and the expansion of "rights-limiting" legislation. In her presentation to Putin, Pamfilova highlighted terrorist acts, the increase in drug use and alcohol consumption, the spread of HIV, car accidents, uncontrolled illegal migration inflows, inefficient state supervision of the construction industry, and widespread corruption as the major problems leading to the violations of fundamental human rights in the country.

According to the 2015 ombudsman's report, the Ombudsman's Office received 64,189 complaints from individuals, state organizations, and NGOs during the year, representing an 18 percent increase in complaints compared with 2014. The country has regional ombudsmen in 83 of its 85 regions with responsibilities similar to Moskalkova's. Their effectiveness varied significantly, and local authorities often undermined their independence.

Section 6. Discrimination, Societal Abuses, and Trafficking in Persons

Women

Rape and Domestic Violence: Rape is illegal, and the law provides the same punishment for a relative, including the spouse, who commits rape as for a nonrelative. Rape victims may act as full legal parties in criminal cases brought against alleged assailants and may seek compensation as part of a court verdict without initiating a separate civil action. While members of the medical profession assisted assault survivors and sometimes helped identify an assault or rape case, doctors were often reluctant to provide testimony in court.

The penalty for rape is three- to six-years' imprisonment for a single offender and four to 10 years if a group of persons commits the crime or the assailant had prior convictions for sexual assault. Violations are punishable by eight to 15 years in prison if the victim was between the ages of 14 and 18 and by 12 to 20 years in prison if the victim died or was under 14. According to NGOs, many law enforcement personnel and prosecutors did not consider spousal or acquaintance rape a priority and did not encourage reporting or prosecuting such cases. NGOs reported that local police officers sometimes refused to respond to rape or domestic violence calls unless the victim's life was directly threatened.

According to NGOs, many women did not report rape or other violence, especially when committed by spouses, due to social stigma and the lack of government support.

Domestic violence remained a major problem. There is no significant domestic violence provision in the criminal code and no legal definition of domestic violence. The laws that address bodily harm are general in nature and do not permit police to initiate a criminal investigation unless the victim files a complaint.

The burden of collecting evidence in such cases typically falls on the alleged victims. Federal law prohibits battery, assault, threats, and killing, but most acts of domestic violence did not fall within the jurisdiction of the prosecutor's office. According to NGOs police were often unwilling to register complaints of domestic violence and frequently discouraged victims from submitting them.

In February the Duma adopted legislation that removed beating and some other offenses from the criminal code, making them administrative offenses instead. The law's drafters made an exception for so-called "close relatives," keeping beatings of children by parents, between spouses, and between other close persons a criminal, rather than administrative, offense. In June, Children's Rights Ombudsman Pavel Astakhov indicated that the legislative changes providing continued criminal liability for beatings between relatives was "absurd," stating he received a number of complaints from family-focused organizations.

The government does not gather comprehensive data on domestic violence. Ministry of Internal Affairs statistics for 2013 showed that, while women were the victims of 43 percent of all crimes, they were the victims of crimes committed in the home (63 percent), among family members (73 percent), and by a spouse (91 percent) at disproportionately high rates. Additional data from 2013 showed that 60-70 percent of victims did not seek help; and that 97 percent of domestic violence cases did not reach court. According to the BBC, there were 30,600 domestic violence cases in 2014, a 10 percent increase from 2013.

The NGO Center for Women's Support asserted that a majority of domestic violence cases filed with authorities were either dismissed on technical grounds or transferred to a reconciliation process conducted by a justice of the peace, whose focus was on preserving the family rather than punishing the perpetrator. Civil remedies for domestic violence include administrative fines and divorce. Physical harm, property, and family rights cases, such as divorce, asset division, and child custody, cannot be heard in the same case or the same court. No unified court considers civil and criminal cases jointly.

Female Genital Mutilation/Cutting (FGM/C): FGM/C is not specifically prohibited in the criminal code. Local NGOs in Dagestan reported that FGM/C was occasionally practiced in some villages. In August the mufti of the North Caucasus region of Karachayevo-Cherkessia, Ismail Berdiyev, stated that FGM/C was a "Dagestani ritual" and was necessary to "limit unnecessary energy" of future brides. Berdiyev's statement came days after Moscow-based NGO Legal Initiative released a report on FGM/C in Dagestan, which cited some clerics who supported and some who condemned the practice. Later in August, Berdiyev retracted his comments after they resulted in a public outcry and backlash from the country's top Muslim cleric and the Ministry of Health, although some, including a former spokesperson of the Russian Orthodox Church, came out in support of the earlier remarks.

Other Harmful Traditional Practices: According to human rights groups, so-called honor killings of women in Chechnya, Dagestan, and elsewhere in the North Caucasus district continued. Human rights groups further reported that such killings were underreported and rarely prosecuted because of community collusion to cover up such crimes, although there were instances in which such killings led to convictions. According to Interfax, a criminal case was initiated on March 23 against a man in Dagestan accused of stabbing and killing his two daughters for "amoral behavior." According to law enforcement authorities, the man killed his daughters in December 2015 because they came home too late at night. The case was still pending.

In some parts of the North Caucasus, women continued to face bride kidnapping, polygamy, forced marriage (including child marriage), legal discrimination, and enforced adherence to Islamic dress codes. In February a police officer in the North Caucasus was stabbed when he attempted to prevent a bride kidnapping of a 17-year-old girl, according to the Investigative Committee. When the girl's family attempted to prevent the kidnapping, the family of the bride kidnapper would not allow them to enter the home. There were cases in some parts of the North Caucasus where men, claiming that kidnapping brides was an ancient local tradition, reportedly abducted and raped young women, in some cases forcing them into marriage. Police in Dagestan claimed that many cases of women being abducted were in fact voluntary. NGOs reported that, while the overwhelming majority of bride kidnappings were not voluntary, women in the North Caucasus sometimes agreed to be abducted to avoid an arranged marriage, often to an older man or to a man with multiple wives.

Sexual Harassment: The law does not specifically prohibit sexual harassment in the workplace, which remained a widespread problem. Instead, the criminal code contains a general provision against compelling a person to perform actions of a sexual character by means of blackmail, threats, or by taking advantage of the victim's economic or other dependence on the perpetrator. As of April there were 16 successful prosecutions for "compulsion to perform sexual actions" with adults and 34 with minors.

Reproductive Rights: The government recognizes the basic right of couples and individuals to decide the number, spacing, and timing of their children; manage their reproductive health; and have access to the information and means to do so. While there are no legal restrictions on access to contraceptives, the Russian Orthodox Church and the Muftis Council continued their opposition to family planning initiatives, and access to family planning in the country was limited, especially outside big cities. In June authorities banned the leading condom brand in the country, the British brand Durex, for "not being registered in the proper manner." Durex condoms made up one-fourth of the condom market in the country. The ban came just after a government-sponsored study asserted that the main reason for the spread of HIV in the country was condoms (see section 6, HIV and AIDS Social Stigma). Senior government leaders explicitly encouraged women to have as many children as possible to counteract the country's declining population, particularly among ethnic Russians.

Discrimination: The constitution and law provide that men and women enjoy the same legal status and rights. Men and women have an equal right to obtain a bank loan, but women often encountered significant restrictions. There were reports that women encountered discrimination in employment (see section 7.d.).

The law upholds equal ownership rights for women and men. The civil code provides equal rights to access to land and access to other property for men and women. Unless their marriage contract states otherwise, all property acquired during a marriage is the couple's joint property, and it is divided into two equal shares in the event of divorce. Each spouse retains ownership and management of property acquired before marriage or inherited after marriage.

Traditional practices in the North Caucasus award the husband custody of children and all property in divorce cases. As a result, women in the region were often unwilling to seek divorce, even in cases of abuse.

Children

Birth Registration: By law citizenship derives from parents at birth or from birth within the country's territory if the parents are unknown or if the child cannot claim the parents' citizenship. Newborns generally were registered at the local civil registry office where the parents live. A parent must apply for registration within one month of the birth. Birth certificates were issued on the basis of the medical certificate of the hospital where a baby was born.

Education: Education is free and compulsory through grade 11. Regional authorities frequently denied school access to the children of persons who were not registered as residents of the locality, including Roma, asylum seekers, and migrant workers.

Child Abuse: Children's Ombudsman Pavel Astakhov reported an increase in crimes against minors in 2015. The number of minors recognized as victims in 2015 was 102,608, an 8 percent increase over 2014. The number of crimes against the life and health of minors increased 11 percent to 33,525, while the number of sexual crimes against minors increased to 12,175, a more than 20 percent increase over 2014. According to Investigative Committee spokesman Vladimir Markin, there was an increase in child victims of crime in 2015 over the prior year. There were almost 17,000 child victims of crime in 2015, more than 4,600 of whom were under the age of 10. In 2015 authorities filed 10,500 criminal cases involving crimes against minors, 25 percent more than in 2014. Markin reported that 2,300 criminal cases were filed for crimes against children during the first quarter of 2016. In those cases, 4,477 children were identified as victims, 477 of whom had been killed.

During the first quarter of the year, 519 minors were victims of criminal abuse by relatives, including 322 cases of abuse by parents. The Ministry of Internal Affairs published data on 576,000 criminal proceedings filed against parents in 2014 for crimes against children. These included 440,000 cases of negligence, 1,400 for enabling alcohol or drug abuse, and 11,900 cases of physical child abuse, which resulted in more than 2,500 fatalities. In addition 946 of these crimes were cases of pedophilia, 380 of which a parental guardian committed, according to Astakhov. Astakhov reported 8,000 convictions for child abuse in 2015.

According to a 2011 report published by the NGO Foundation for Assistance to Children in Difficult Life Situations, 2,000 to 2,500 children died annually from domestic violence. A 2013 estimate by the Ministry of Internal Affairs indicated that one in four children in the country was subjected to abuse by a parent or foster parent.

Early and Forced Marriage: The minimum legal age for marriage is 18 for both men and women. Local authorities may authorize marriage from the age of 16 under certain circumstances, and even earlier in some regions. In May 2015 the newspaper *Novaya Gazeta* reported that a 17-year-old girl had been pressured into marrying the 57-year-old police chief in Chechnya's Nozhay-Yurt district who was already married. Chechnya head Kadyrov attended the wedding while Children's Ombudsman Astakhov publicly defended such practices in the Caucasus.

Female Genital Mutilation/Cutting: See information for girls under 18 in the women's section above.

Sexual Exploitation of Children: The age of consent is 16. Children, particularly orphans and those without homes, were exploited for child pornography. While authorities considered child pornography to be a serious problem, the law does not criminalize its possession or provide for effective investigation and prosecution of it. The law prohibits the manufacture, distribution, and possession with intent to distribute of child pornography, but possession without intent to distribute is not prohibited by law. Manufacture and distribution of pornography involving children under 18 is punishable by two to eight years in prison, or three to 10 years in prison if it involves children under 14.

In June a definition of child pornography came into force for the first time. The new definition states that child pornography is a whole or partial image or description of the genitalia of a minor, made with "sexual intent," as well as the portrayal of a real or simulated sexual act with a minor or an adult who presents him or herself as a minor. Materials used for educational or medical purposes are not considered child pornography, nor are materials that have historical, artistic, or cultural value. Investigation of child pornography cases are to be turned over from the Ministry for Internal Affairs to the Investigative Committee. In the past courts often dismissed criminal cases because of the lack of clear standards or definitions, and authorities had not determined how the new legal provisions defining child pornography would be enforced in the coming year.

The Investigative Committee reported filing charges in 1,645 cases of rape against children in 2015 as well as in more than 5,300 cases of sexual assault of children. According to Ministry of Internal Affairs statistics, in 2014 the ministry opened 274 investigative cases into child pornography and referred 80 of these to the courts. In addition to its authority to regulate websites containing extremist materials, Roskomnadzor has the power to shut down any website immediately and without due process until its owners prove its content does not include child pornography. In 2014 approximately 15 percent of the 45,700 links Roskomnadzor shut down were related to child pornography.

Displaced Children: Official statistics on the numbers of orphans and displaced children in the country were conflicting and of questionable reliability. In 2014 the

Ministry of Education and Science estimated there were 96,000 orphans in the country, down from a previous estimate of 120,000. In May 2015 Children's Ombudsman Astakhov announced that the number of orphans without parental supervision had declined from 106,700 in 2009 to 61,600 in 2014. In March, Deputy Prime Minister Olga Golodets announced there were 53,100 homeless children who had run away from home in 2014, a 22 percent increase from 2013. No recent official statistics on the number of parentless migrants were available. A 2011 study conducted by the Ministry of Education's Center for Sociological Research indicated that 45 percent of homeless and unaccompanied children in Moscow were migrant children from member countries of the Commonwealth of Independent States.

Homeless children often engaged in criminal activities, received no education, and were vulnerable to substance abuse. Some children on the streets were forced into prostitution. Law enforcement officers reportedly abused street children, blamed them for unsolved crimes, and committed illegal acts against them, including extortion, detention, and psychological and sexual violence.

Regional ombudsmen for children operated in all the country's regions. They had the authority to conduct independent investigations involving violations of children's rights, inspect all institutions and executive offices dealing with minors, establish councils of public experts, and conduct independent evaluations of legislation affecting children. A number of schools in the Moscow and Volgograd oblasts had school ombudsmen to deal with children and families and identify potential conflicts and violations of children's rights.

Institutionalized Children: In January media reported accusations by students in a boarding school in Bratsk, Irkutsk Region, of physical abuse by guards, including the use of electric shocks. There were other reports of physical, sexual, and psychological abuse in state institutions for children.

According to the Prosecutor General's Office, graduates of state orphanages and boarding schools faced grim futures. The office reported that only 10 percent of graduates adapted successfully, while 40 percent committed crimes, 40 percent become addicted to alcohol and drugs, and 10 percent committed suicide. The office reported that 300,000 "socially dangerous acts" were committed by children each year, of which 100,000 were committed by children under the age of criminal responsibility (14).

International Child Abductions: The country is a party to the 1980 Hague Convention on the Civil Aspects of International Child Abduction. See the Department of State's *Annual Report on International Parental Child Abduction* at travel.state.gov/content/childabduction/en/legal/compliance.html.

Anti-Semitism

The 2010 census estimated the Jewish population at just over 150,000. In February 2015, however, the president of the Federation of Jewish Communities of Russia stated that the actual Jewish population was nearly one million.

A number of leading figures in the Jewish community reported the level of anti-Semitism in the country was decreasing and that anti-Semitism was primarily manifested in anti-Semitic rhetoric on state television channels. There was also anti-Semitism reported in the security services, and anti-Semitic literature could be found distributed around the country.

According to a report by the Kantor Center for the Study of Contemporary European Jewry at Tel Aviv University, eight cases of aggressive anti-Semitism were recorded in the country in 2015. The Kantor Center also noted, however, that anti-Semitism in the country was mainly expressed in the form of propaganda. The center identified the newspaper *Komsomolskaya Pravda* and the state-funded RT television network as a "main stage for virulent anti-Semitic and anti-Israeli propaganda." The conflict between Russia and Ukraine in particular led to a rise in anti-Semitic propaganda, with "each side blaming the other for using it as a political tool."

Rabbi Alexander Boroda, president of the Federation of Jewish Communities of Russia, condemned as anti-Semitic the RT channel's June 27 airing of Palestinian allegations that an Israeli rabbi approved the poisoning of Palestinian wells. In June the SOVA Center reported on a series of anti-Semitic articles published in Saratov that attempted to discredit stories of Jewish heroism during the Second World War and arouse hostility towards Jews.

On April 10, Vladislav Vikhorev, a candidate for Putin's United Russia party, who was campaigning for a seat in the Chelyabinsk Oblast legislative assembly, was quoted by the news website *Apostroph* as stating that Jews in the 1990s were behind a "Jewish revolution that put Russian sovereignty itself on the brink of extinction." He claimed Jews had "a well-planned, well-designed program of destruction of national culture, national education, national production, and the national financial system." In response, Chief Rabbi Berel Lazar called on the government to stamp out hate speech against Jews. The local election committee issued Vikhorev a warning but allowed him to maintain his candidacy.

On October 2, police arrested a man who attacked a synagogue in Moscow, injuring a guard and attempting to set fire to the building while shouting anti-Semitic slogans.

On June 12, in one of a series of attacks on social media network users of VKontakte, unidentified men attacked a VKontakte employee known for his occasional antigovernment posts. The attackers broke three of his fingers and called their victim a "traitor," a "Jew," and a member of the "fifth column"--a term frequently used by Russian state media to describe the opposition.

In November the Levada Center published a survey, conducted in Russia in 2015, indicating that 8 percent of respondents expressed negative feelings about Jews, compared with 13 percent in 1992 and 16 percent in 1997.

Nationalist marches on November 4 included banners in support of national socialism along with imagery and slogans that were implicitly linked to Nazism.

The government investigated anti-Semitic crimes, and some courts placed anti-Semitic literature on the Ministry of Justice's list of banned extremist materials.

Trafficking in Persons

See the Department of State's *Trafficking in Persons Report* at www.state.gov/j/tip/rls/tiprpt/.

Persons with Disabilities

While several laws prohibit discrimination against persons with physical, sensory, intellectual, and mental disabilities in employment, education, transportation, access to health care, and the provision of state services, the government generally did not enforce these laws. No laws prohibit discrimination in air travel.

Persons with disabilities continued to face discrimination and denial of equal access to education, employment, and social institutions. Persons with mental disabilities were subject to severe discrimination in education and employment (see section 7.d.). In addition the conditions of guardianship imposed by courts deprived them of almost all personal rights. Under the family code, individuals with mental disabilities were at times prevented from getting married without a guardian's consent. According to HRW, although the government has begun to implement inclusive education, most children with disabilities did not study in mainstream schools due to a lack of reasonable accommodations to facilitate their individual learning needs. The lack of reasonable accommodations left tens of thousands of children with disabilities isolated at home or in specialized schools, often far from their homes. Most children with disabilities in orphanages had at least one living parent, and many faced violence and neglect, including inadequate health care, education, and opportunities to play, according to HRW.

In July local registry officials in Nizhny Novgorod denied a marriage license to a blind couple arguing that neither the bride nor groom could independently sign the documents.

On March 29, the ECHR, in a landmark ruling, found that the government should not have denied Vitaliy Kocherov custody of his daughter for the first six years of her life solely because both he and his wife have mental disabilities.

Conditions in institutions for adults with disabilities were often poor, with unqualified staff and overcrowding. Institutions rarely attempted to develop the abilities of residents, whom they frequently confined to the premises and whose movements they sometimes restricted within the institutions themselves.

On January 1, new amendments to the law for the social protection of persons with disabilities became effective. The amendments broaden the criteria for establishing a person's disability, introduce a federal register of persons with disabilities, require barrier-free accessibility, and access to social services. Under the previous system introduced by Ministry of Labor and Social Protection in 2015, grant benefits for the persons with disabilities were changed based on the type of medical condition and the extensiveness of the symptoms. The changes affected hundreds of thousands of individuals who were denied disability benefits during the year based on the new requirements. Under the system only persons deemed to have lost at least 40 percent of one of their body functions could apply for financial assistance. The January amendments restored many of the previous categories of disabilities.

Federal law requires that buildings be accessible to persons with disabilities, but authorities did not enforce the law, and many buildings were not accessible. In a 2013 report, HRW noted that, in apartment buildings constructed before 2001 (that is, prior to the development of minimum accessibility standards for new construction), doorways and elevators were too narrow for wheelchairs and buildings lacked elevators or appropriate ramps. In some cases buildings constructed after 2001 also lacked these accommodations. This lack of building access was an insurmountable barrier to employment, education, and social engagement for the vast majority of wheelchair users interviewed in the report. The report also noted that critical public facilities and emergency services remained largely inaccessible to persons with disabilities. Disability rights NGOs confirmed that accessibility remained a problem, noting that only a handful of Moscow's 200 subway stations had elevators to accommodate patrons with disabilities.

In July a man with disabilities from Krasnoyarsk committed suicide after local authorities refused to install a wheelchair ramp at his residence. According to media reports, the man had been confined to his home for the previous three years due to lack of accessibility. His mother told media that authorities continually denied requests for the ramp and told her son the city could not install the ramp until 2038.

Most children with disabilities remained isolated from other community members and were unable to attend public schools, since only 3 percent of schools could accommodate them. According to a 2014 HRW report, nearly 30 percent of all children with disabilities lived in state orphanages, where they faced violence and neglect. Some children interviewed by HRW reported that orphanage staff beat them, injected them with sedatives, and sent them to psychiatric hospitals for days or weeks at a time to control or punish them.

HRW reported that at least 95 percent of children living in orphanages and foster care had at least one living parent, although children with disabilities who entered institutions at a young age were unlikely to return to their birth families, mostly due to the practice of local-level state commissions recommending continued institutionalization of children. Staff working in institutions that HRW visited occasionally discouraged visits or other contact with family members, claiming that such contact "spoiled" children by getting them accustomed to too much attention. Within orphanages, HRW documented the segregation of children whom staff deemed to have the most severe disabilities into "lying-down" rooms, where they were confined to cribs and often tied to furniture with rags. Many of these children received little attention except for feeding and diaper changing.

According to Ministry of Internal Affairs data, more than 45 percent of the country's total population of children with disabilities were institutionalized. While the law mandates inclusive education for children with disabilities, authorities generally segregated them from mainstream society through a system that institutionalized them through adulthood. Graduates of such institutions often lacked the necessary social, educational, and vocational skills to function in society.

There were numerous cases of child abuse in state facilities. The Prosecutor General's Office requested a criminal investigation into a youth facility in Dagestan after allegations of abuse surfaced in March. According to media, former orphanage pupils reported that children, many with disabilities, were forced to sleep on the floor and that they received injections from staff to make them sleep. There were also allegations that children were forced to shower as a group in cold water.

There appeared to be no legal mechanism by which individuals could contest their assignment to a facility for persons with disabilities. The classification of children with mental disabilities to categories of disability often followed them through their lives. The official designations "imbecile" and "idiot," assigned by a commission that assesses children with developmental problems at the age of three, signify that authorities considered a child uneducable. These designations were almost always irrevocable. The designation "weak" (having a slight cognitive or intellectual disability) followed an individual on official documents, creating barriers to employment and housing after graduation from state institutions.

During the World Ice Hockey Championship in May, police in St. Petersburg refused to allow a man with cerebral palsy into the match because they did not like his manner of walking.

Election laws do not specifically mandate that polling places be accessible to persons with disabilities, and the majority of polling stations were not. Election officials generally brought mobile ballot boxes to the homes of voters with disabilities.

National/Racial/Ethnic Minorities

The law prohibits discrimination based on nationality, but government officials increasingly subjected minorities to discrimination. According to the SOVA

Center, as of July racial violence resulted in the death of at least one person, while 32 others were injured, and two received death threats. Incidents were reported in eight regions, although the violence tended to be concentrated in Moscow and St. Petersburg. Skinhead groups and other extreme nationalist organizations fomented racially motivated violence. Racist propaganda remained a problem, although courts continued to convict individuals of using propaganda to incite ethnic hatred.

As was the case in 2015, there were fewer reports of skinhead violence than in previous years. The Ministry of Justice added a number of skinhead videos found on social media, as well as skinhead, ultranationalist, and xenophobic publications, to the *Federal List of Extremist Materials*.

Nationalist organizations held a number of rallies throughout the year, but due to continued law enforcement pressure on nationalist groups, there were drastically lower levels of public activity. A May 2 demonstration in Moscow held by the nationalist group Committee of January 25 to commemorate clashes in 2014 between Euromaidan and anti-Maidan protesters in Odessa, Ukraine, drew between 250 and 300 persons. Most nationalist events during the year, however, drew significantly fewer participants. On July 7, the National-Conservative Movement and the Union of Orthodox Banner Bearers held a rally in Moscow in memory of the Russian royal family executed in 1918. The campaign attracted no more than 20 participants from Orthodox and monarchist groups.

Incidents highlighted longstanding discrimination against Roma and tensions between the Romani community and authorities. On March 17, residents of a Romani settlement in Tula clashed with riot police over access to a gas pipeline running through their community. Romani residents had been siphoning gas illegally from the pipeline for years because authorities had refused to give Romani families legal title to their land and allow them to register for gas service. The overwhelmed pipeline eventually broke down, and when engineers came to repair it, Romani residents attempted to block them so they would not cut off their access to gas. The incident turned violent, with children wielding sticks at police, who put down the protest with force.

In some cases authorities held perpetrators responsible for xenophobic violence, and there were at least 16 convictions for such acts as of July, resulting in the sentencing of 40 persons to prison terms for hate crimes. This included 12 members of the Moscow neo-Nazi group 14/88 who were sentenced to prison terms of between four and 10 years for racially motivated murder and other violent crimes.

Police and migration officials continued to engage in anti-immigrant raids in markets, factories, the subway, and city streets. GAMI/the FMS organized civilian patrols in which volunteers could sign up to participate in such raids under the supervision of migration service officials.

Grassroots ultra right activists also conducted raids during the year targeting suspected irregular or undocumented migrants. On July 22 in St. Petersburg, six or seven individuals belonging to a Cossack group entered a construction area that was home to migrant workers from Central Asia, broke down the doors, dragged 40 persons outside, and turned them over to police. In April in Moscow, the National-Conservative Movement conducted a raid in which its members checked shawarma sellers for their registration and certificates of production.

Right-wing activists capitalized on the high-profile killing of a five-year-old girl by her Uzbek nanny to promote prejudice against Muslims and anti-immigrant policies. On February 29, Gulchekhra Bobokulovaya decapitated the child in her care and waved the severed head at a busy metro station while shouting, "Allahu akbar" and threatening to blow herself up. In addition to the incident's exploitation by right-wing groups, the Moscow City council of the Communist Party put the graphic image of the event on a party poster and called for several discriminatory measures, including a visa regime with Central Asian countries and a lifetime entry ban on foreigners who have committed a crime in Russia.

Indigenous People

The constitution and various statutes provide support for "small-numbered" indigenous peoples of the North, Siberia, and the Far East, permitting them to create self-governing bodies and allowing them to seek compensation if economic development threatens their lands. The government granted the status of "indigenous" and associated benefits only to those ethnic groups numbering fewer than 50,000 and maintaining their traditional way of life. Small-numbered indigenous groups throughout the country (including the Udege in the Far East, the Khanty in Siberia, and the Chukchi in the North) continued to work actively to preserve and defend their cultures as well as their right to benefit from the economic resources in their regions. The majority of small-numbered indigenous communities believed that a combination of overlapping legal codes and authorities' lack of political will to enforce existing laws prevented them from fully exercising their rights.

Most members of indigenous communities asserted that they received the same treatment as ethnic Russians, although some more vocal activists claimed they were either unrepresented or underrepresented in regional governments and that the government failed to address seriously the problems of indigenous communities in recent decades. Small-numbered indigenous groups also expressed concern that they lacked adequate representation in the federal government. In 2015 responsibility for indigenous issues shifted from the Ministry of Culture to the newly created Federal Agency for Nationalities. During the year the government introduced fishing restrictions and eliminated special quotas for indigenous peoples throughout the country, endangering some communities in Khabarovsk and Kamchatka that depend on fishing.

The Russian Association of Indigenous Peoples of the North (RAIPON), the country's largest NGO for indigenous persons, represented 41 groups spread across the country with approximately 250,000 members. In 2013 government pressure led to the rejection of the candidacy of respected activist Pavel Sulyandziga to become RAIPON's president and to a subsequent political purge of RAIPON's leadership. Although Sulyandziga agreed to stay on as first vice president, a Duma member from the ruling United Russia party, Grigoriy Ledkov, was installed as president. Sulyandziga stepped down in early 2016 over disagreements with Ledkov over indigenous policy and corruption.

Indigenous contacts reported an increase in state-sponsored harassment, including interrogations by the security services, as well as employment discrimination (see section 7.d).

Since 2015 the Ministry of Justice has added several NGOs focusing on indigenous issues to the foreign agents' list. In November 2015 the Center for Support of Indigenous Peoples of the North, an NGO headed by Rodion Sulyandziga, the brother of Pavel Sulyandziga, was added to the list. According to the ministry's website, the center engaged in political activity while receiving foreign funding from the World Bank, the UN Democracy Fund, and the Danish-based International Work Group for Indigenous Affairs. On March 11, the Ministry of Justice designated the Batani International Foundation for the Development of Indigenous and Small Numbered Peoples of the North, Siberia, and Far East (aka Batani Fund) as a foreign agent. The Batani Fund was headed by Pavel Sulyandziga and listed its mission as protecting the rights of indigenous and small numbered peoples.

Pavel Sulyandziga told media outlets that his confrontations with officials from the Ministry of Regional Development over his attempts to enforce the rights of indigenous persons to receive their hunting and fishing quotas were the reason his organization was added to the foreign agents' list. Pavel Sulyandziga criticized the government's approach to supporting indigenous people as simply providing funding for indigenous festivals and holidays but not allowing them the use of rivers or traditional land sites. In August the Tengri School of Spiritual Ecology in the Altai Republic, which promoted environmental protection and ethnic culture in the region, was also forced to register as a foreign agent.

Acts of Violence, Discrimination, and Other Abuses Based on Sexual Orientation and Gender Identity

The law criminalizes the distribution of "propaganda" of nontraditional sexual relations to minors and effectively limits the rights of free expression and assembly for citizens who wish to advocate publicly for rights or express the opinion that homosexuality is normal. Examples of what the government considered LGBTI propaganda included materials that "directly or indirectly approve of persons who are in nontraditional sexual relationships." Antidiscrimination laws exist but do not explicitly prohibit discrimination based on sexual orientation or gender identity. Authorities rarely investigated cases of physical violence against LGBTI persons as hate crimes.

During the year there were reports of killings motivated by the sexual orientation or gender identity of the victim. On March 31, a journalist and well-known arts and theater critic, Dmitriy Tsilikin, was found dead with multiple stab injuries in his home in St. Petersburg. Police arrested suspect Sergey Kosyrev, who admitted that he had met Tsilikin online and planned to blackmail him for his presumed homosexuality, but killed him in a quarrel. Media reports indicated that Kosyrev, who was charged with Tsilikin's killing, had expressed support for neo-Nazi ideology on social media.

On February 1, a transgender woman named Angela Likina was stabbed to death by one of her neighbors in Ufa. Likina came to prominence after a video on social media showed a traffic police officer laughing uncontrollably with his partner after examining her documents and releasing her upon discovering that she was transgender. Likina expressed dismay about the release of the video and the attention it garnered. The alleged perpetrator was detained.

Human rights groups reported continuing violence against LGBTI individuals. Openly gay men were particular targets of attacks, and police often failed to respond adequately to such incidents. On June 12, a group of nine soccer fans savagely beat visitors to the Mono gay club in Yekaterinburg; one victim suffered a concussion and a broken leg. Police responded to the scene but failed to search the surrounding area for the attackers, even though witnesses told police where to look. Yekaterinburg authorities stated they were investigating.

There were reports that police abused and harassed individuals whom they perceived to be LGBTI. A report released by the LGBT Network in March documented 21 cases of alleged violations of LGBTI person's rights by law enforcement officials during 2015. In one case, on July 11, police in Krasnodar reportedly harassed, detained, and threatened a man with rape based on his presumed sexual orientation. Authorities subsequently charged him with refusing to obey police orders and sentenced him to pay a fine. Human rights groups were appealing the court's decision.

On June 13, police arrested two men, Islam Abdullabekov and Felix Glyukman, after they placed a sign that read "Love wins" at a memorial in Moscow for the victims of the shooting at a gay nightclub in Orlando. Authorities charged the men with holding an unauthorized demonstration and questioned them for three hours before releasing them. If convicted, they each face up to 10 days in prison or a fine of 60,000 rubles ($900).

LGBTI activists experienced threats and attacks by private individuals. On August 6, a private sports event organized by the Russia LGBT Sports Federation at a campground in Nizhny Novgorod was attacked by persons who beat participants with sticks while shouting homophobic insults. Three persons were injured in the attack. Police opened an investigation.

LGBTI individuals often declined to report attacks against them due to fears that police would subject them to mistreatment or publicize their sexual orientation or gender identity. In May the newspaper *Meduza* reported that a criminal gang in St. Petersburg lured gay men on fake dates in order to beat and rob them. The robbers correctly presumed that few victims would report the crimes to police.

On July 7, LGBTI activist Violetta Grudina complained to the ECHR that authorities failed to carry out an effective investigation into an attack on the Maximum Center for Social, Psychological, and Legal Assistance to Victims of Homophobia and Discrimination in Murmansk ("Maximum"). In April 2015 assailants sprayed suffocating gas into the center, injuring two persons. Police refused to open a criminal investigation. "Maximum" was liquidated in October 2015 after being designated a foreign agent.

There were reports that authorities restricted the freedoms of expression, association, and assembly of individuals who expressed support for the human rights of LGBTI persons. Authorities invoked the law prohibiting the distribution of propaganda of nontraditional sexual relations to minors to restrict the free speech of LGBTI persons and their supporters, which contributed to an environment of self-censorship among media outlets, rights organizations, and others on LGBTI problems. For example, on January 18, a Murmansk court fined the former leader of the LGBTI organization "Maximum," Sergey Alekseyenko, 100,000 rubles ($1,500) for violating the "propaganda" law by posting positive views of LGBTI persons and relationships on the organization's website on the social network VKontakte. One of the postings deemed "propaganda" was a poem by the 19th century Russian writer Mikhail Lermontov that described a sexual scene between two young men. The other posting was nearly an exact quote from a complaint that Roskomnadzor filed against the LGBTI group Deti 404 that read, "Children! To be gay means to be a person who is brave, strong, confident, persistent, who has a sense of dignity and self-respect." Alekseyenko was the fifth LGBTI activist prosecuted under the "gay propaganda law."

On March 1, the Ministry of Justice added the St. Petersburg NGO Sfera, which provided social and legal services to members of the LGBTI community, to the list of foreign agents. Sfera was at least the third LGBTI organization placed on the foreign agents' list. Two other groups were listed in 2015: "Maximum" and Rakurs, an LGBTI advocacy organization based in Arkhangelsk.

Many events planned by members of the LGBTI community were officially unsanctioned and conducted in private due to security concerns. Nevertheless, the LGBT Network reported that in at least four cases during the year LGBTI-related events were disrupted, sometimes through anonymous calls alleging bomb threats.

Moscow authorities refused to allow a gay pride parade for the 11th consecutive year, despite a 2010 ECHR ruling that the denial violated the rights to freedom of assembly and freedom from discrimination. In February the ECHR agreed to review two cases brought by representatives of the country's LGBTI community on the prohibition of more than a hundred public events across the country between 2009 and 2015.

On May 1, police in St. Petersburg detained approximately 20 LGBTI activists after they unfurled a rainbow flag at the annual May Day parade. Authorities had banned LGBTI groups from participating in the event two days prior to the march. This was the first time that authorities had prohibited LGBTI groups from taking part in the event; an estimated 600 demonstrators marched with LGBTI groups during the 2015 parade. According to the organizers, Roskomnadzor blocked access to the group's official website and VKontakte page ahead of the event.

A homophobic campaign continued in state-controlled media, in which officials, journalists, and others called LGBTI persons "perverts," "sodomites," and "abnormal" and conflated homosexuality with pedophilia.

LGBTI persons reported heightened societal stigma and discrimination, which some attributed to increasing official promotion of intolerance and homophobia. Activists asserted that the majority of LGBTI persons hid their sexual orientation or gender identity due to fear of losing their jobs or homes as well as the threat of violence. Medical practitioners reportedly continued to limit or deny LGBTI persons health services due to intolerance and prejudice. There were reports that high levels of employment discrimination against LGBTI persons persisted (see section 7.d.) and that LGBTI persons continued to seek asylum abroad due to the domestic environment.

Although the law allows transgender individuals to change their names and gender classifications on government documents, they faced difficulties because the government had not established standard procedures and many civil registry offices denied their requests. When their documents failed to reflect their gender accurately, transgender persons often faced harassment by law enforcement officers and discrimination in accessing health care, education, housing, transportation, and employment. In one case in February, a transgender woman named Alina Davis was sentenced to two months in a men's prison for driving with a fake license because her documents identified her as male. Transgender activists advocated for authorities to take steps that would fully legalize sex reassignment surgery and clarify procedures for changing gender identity on official documents.

There were some isolated positive developments during the year for the LGBTI community. For the first time in its eight-year history, the international LGBTI pride festival of Russia, Queerfest, took place in St. Petersburg in September without attacks or harassment. The event drew more than 1,500 persons. Other LGBTI-related events, such as an annual sports festival in St. Petersburg in March and a photography exhibit in Moscow in August, were held throughout the country.

There were rare instances in which courts found in favor of LGBTI persons seeking to exercise their human rights. In March the Kostroma City Court ruled that the city should pay Nikolay Alekseyev, founder of the Moscow Gay Pride Parade movement, 6,600 rubles ($99) in compensation for banning a gay pride parade there in 2014. On July 29, a Novosibirsk court ruled that Anna Balash had been subjected to discrimination by the company Sib-Alians, which had twice refused her employment on the grounds of "nontraditional sexual orientation." The court ordered Sib-Alians to pay Balash 1,000 rubles ($15) compensation.

HIV and AIDS Social Stigma

Persons with HIV/AIDS faced significant legal discrimination, informal stigma-based barriers, and employment discrimination (see section 7.d.) and were prohibited from adopting children. In addition, intravenous drug users in particular faced informal barriers to accessing antiretroviral treatment. Regional AIDS centers often demanded that drug users complete drug addiction treatment, which was severely lacking or nonexistent in most areas, before starting antiretroviral treatment.

According to NGO activists, men who have sex with men were discouraged from seeking antiretroviral treatment, since treatment exposed the fact that these individuals have the virus, while sex workers were afraid to appear in the official system due to threats from law enforcement bodies. Economic migrants also concealed their HIV status and avoided treatment due to fear of deportation. By law foreign citizens who are HIV positive may be deported. The law, however, bars the deportation of HIV-positive foreigners who have a Russian national or permanent resident spouse, child (including adopted children), or parents (including adoptive parents).

Prisoners with HIV/AIDS experienced regular abuse and denial of medical treatment.

Although the law provides for treatment of HIV-positive persons, drug shortages, legal barriers, and lack of funds caused large gaps in treatment. Regional AIDS centers continued to force patients to take "vacations" from antiretrovirals for three months due to drug shortages, according to the NGO Patients Control. In September 2015 a Moscow court ruled that the Moscow AIDS Center could refuse to provide antiretroviral drugs to temporary residents in the city. According to NGOs, temporary residents were often told to return to their location of permanent residency for treatment (changing one's permanent residence is administratively difficult and often requires property ownership or family ties).

In May a government-backed study by the Russian Institute for Strategic Research asserted that condoms are the main reason for the HIV epidemic in the country. The study's scientists suggested that the best way to protect against HIV is to "be in a heterosexual family where both partners are loyal to each other."

The Ministry of Justice cracked down on HIV-related NGOs, adding seven to the foreign agents' list, effectively shutting them down. In one example, in August the Ministry of Justice added Panacea, a youth NGO dedicated to combatting the spread of HIV, to the register of foreign agents. Based in Kuznetsk, Penza region (approximately 150 miles west of Samara), Panacea focused on youth HIV prevention by providing condoms and clean syringes to "at risk" residents. Prosecutors alleged that Panacea's activities, including the distribution of condoms and syringes, conflicted with public policy on drug abuse and AIDS prevention. The prosecutors asserted that the activities could not be considered humanitarian or ideological and were "political" in nature. Panacea worked closely with the NGO ESVERO, a union of organizations involved in HIV prevention, that was added to the list of foreign agents in June.

Other Societal Violence or Discrimination

The lack of an internal passport often prevented homeless citizens from fully securing their legal rights and social services. Homeless persons faced barriers to obtaining legal documentation.

Section 7. Worker Rights

a. Freedom of Association and the Right to Collective Bargaining

The law provides that workers may form and join independent unions, bargain collectively, and conduct legal strikes. The law prohibits antiunion discrimination, but it does not require employers to reinstate workers fired due to their union activity. The law prohibits reprisals against striking workers. Unions must register with the Federal Registration Service, often a cumbersome process that included lengthy delays and convoluted bureaucracy. The grounds on which trade union registration may be denied are not defined and could be arbitrary or unjustified.

The law requires labor unions to be independent of government bodies, employers, political parties, and NGOs.

The law places several restrictions on the right to bargain collectively. For example, only one collective bargaining agreement is permitted per enterprise, and only a union or group of unions representing at least half the workforce may bargain collectively. The law does not specify who has authority to bargain collectively when there is no trade union in an enterprise.

Government policy limited the exercise of freedom of association and collective bargaining. In the summer labor union organizers from Ugra State University were fired after they attempted to establish a union. Their termination came on the heels of the dissolution of the previous labor union, whose leaders had also been terminated, according to the Russian Labor Confederation in September 2016. Similarly, the Confederation of Labor and its member, the Interregional Union of Movie and Radio Workers, late in 2015 claimed the Ministry of Culture had failed to protect the interests of actors. In response to this complaint, the ministry terminated the working group responsible for regulating labor relations between actors and producers.

The labor code prohibits strikes in the military and emergency response services. It also prohibits strikes in essential public-service sectors, including utilities and transportation, and strikes that would threaten the country's defense and safety or the life and health of its workers. The law also prohibits some nonessential public servants from striking and imposes compulsory arbitration for railway, postal, and municipal workers as well as other public servants in roles other than law enforcement.

Extensive legal requirements complicated workers' abilities to exercise the right to strike. According to the Federation of Independent Trade Unions of Russia, the legal preparation for a strike takes at least 40 days. Solidarity strikes and strikes on issues related to state policies are illegal, as are strikes that do not respect the onerous time limits, procedures, and requirements mandated by law. Workers must give prior notice of the following aspects of a proposed strike: a list of the differences of opinion between the parties that triggered the strike; the date and time at which the strike will start, its duration and the number of anticipated participants; the name of the body that is leading the strike and the representatives authorized to participate in the conciliation procedures; and proposals for the minimum service to be provided during the strike. In the event a declared strike continues after it is ruled illegal, courts may confiscate union property to cover employers' losses.

The Federal Labor and Employment Service (RosTrud) regulates employer compliance with labor laws and is responsible for "controlling and supervising compliance with labor laws and other legal acts which deal with labor norms" by employers. Several state agencies including the Ministry of Justice, the Prosecutor's Office, the Federal Service for Labor and Employment, and the Ministry of Internal Affairs are responsible for enforcing the law. These agencies, however, frequently failed to fulfill their responsibilities, and violations of freedom of association were common.

Discrimination against employees and trade union leaders due to their union membership was common, as was pressure against workers to leave, or not to join, unions. Labor activists reported police regularly intimidated union supporters, including by subjecting them to detention and extensive interrogations and provoking physical confrontations with them.

Employers frequently engaged in reprisals against workers for union activity, including threatening to assign them to night shifts, denying benefits, and blacklisting or firing them. For example, although unions were occasionally successful in court, in most cases company managers who engaged in antiunion activities did not face penalties.

b. Prohibition of Forced or Compulsory Labor

The law prohibits most forms of forced or compulsory labor but allows for compulsory labor as a penal sentence, in some cases as labor contracted to private enterprises.

The government did not effectively enforce the law. Men and women were engaged in forced labor in the construction industry, logging industry, textile shops, and agricultural sector (see section 7.c.). Workers experienced exploitative labor conditions characteristic of trafficking cases, such as withholding of identity documents, nonpayment for services rendered, physical abuse, or extremely poor living conditions. Under a state-to-state agreement in effect since 2009, North Korean citizens worked in the country in a variety of sectors, including the logging and construction industries in the Far East. The Federal State Statistics Service, citing GAMI/the FMS numbers, registered 30,000 North Korean workers as of June.

In the first half of the year, the Ministry of Internal Affairs registered 262 cases of unlawful deprivation of liberty, human trafficking, or using slave labor. The criminal code imposes criminal liability against persons depriving another of their "freedom and human dignity," including slave labor and human trafficking. The maximum penalty is a 15-year prison term. Experts noted it was difficult to prove guilt under the statute.

Also see the Department of State's *Trafficking in Persons Report* at www.state.gov/j/tip/rls/tiprpt/.

c. Prohibition of Child Labor and Minimum Age for Employment

The law prohibits the employment of children under the age of 16 in most cases and regulates the working conditions of children younger than 18, including the prohibition of dangerous nighttime and overtime work. The law permits children to work at the age of 14 under certain conditions and with the approval of a parent or guardian. Such work must not threaten the child's health or welfare. The labor code lists occupations that are restricted for children under 18, including work in unhealthy or dangerous conditions, underground work, or jobs that might endanger a child's health and moral development.

RosTrud is responsible for inspecting enterprises and organizations to identify violations of labor and occupational health standards for minors. The government did not effectively enforce the law. Typical violations, such as employing child labor, were classified as administrative violations and were punished with fines that were insufficient to deter violations.

In 2015 regional labor inspectors found 419 child labor violations, compared with 927 in 2014. Information on penalties assessed during the year was not available.

Typical violations included the failure to conclude contracts, overtime work, and failure to assure compliance with health and safety measures. According to the administrative code, fines range from 1,000 to 100,000 rubles ($15 to $1,500). Such violations often recurred year after year, indicating that government action was not sufficient to deter such violations; however, these violations were not severe.

In urban areas children worked primarily in the construction and informal sectors, engaging in retail services, selling goods on the street, washing cars, and making deliveries. In rural areas children worked in agriculture. Some children, both Russian and foreign, were subjected to commercial sexual exploitation (see section 6, Children).

Also see the Department of Labor's *Findings on the Worst Forms of Child Labor* at www.dol.gov/ilab/reports/child-labor/findings/.

d. Discrimination with Respect to Employment and Occupation

The labor code prohibits employment discrimination based on sex, race, skin color, nationality, language, national origin, property, social status or position, age, domicile, religious beliefs, political convictions, affiliation or nonaffiliation with public associations, and other factors not relevant to the professional qualities of the employee. It also requires equal pay for equal work. The law does not prohibit discrimination based on sexual orientation, HIV status, gender identity, or disability. Employment laws were not always effectively enforced, and penalties for violations were insufficient to deter employers from violating the law.

Discrimination based on gender in compensation, professional training, hiring, and dismissal were characteristic of the labor market. Employers often preferred to hire men to save on maternity and child-care costs and avoid the perceived unreliability associated with women with small children. Such discrimination was often very difficult to prove, although NGOs reported several successful lawsuits in St. Petersburg against companies for wrongful termination of women on maternity leave.

A 2013 law prohibits employer discrimination in posting job vacancy information. It also prohibits employers from requesting workers with specific gender, race, nationality, address registration, age, and other factors unrelated to personal skills and competencies. Notwithstanding the law, vacancy announcements continued to specify gender and age requirements, and some also specified a desired physical appearance and preference for applicants who were open to intimate relations with their prospective supervisors. According to the Center for Social and Labor Rights, courts often ruled in favor of employees filing complaints, but the sums awarded were inconsequential. Many employees therefore preferred not to spend the money and time to take legal action.

The labor code restricts women's employment in jobs with "harmful or dangerous conditions or work underground, except in nonphysical jobs or sanitary and consumer services," and forbids women's employment in "manual handling of bulk weights that exceed the set limits for their handling."

The World Bank's *2016 Report on Women, Business, and Law: Getting to Equal*, published in September 2015, documented government restrictions on women's employment numbering in the hundreds, including in the mining, manufacturing, and construction industries, that prohibit women from operating farm machinery, driving trains, or operating cranes at shipyards. According to the World Bank and the UN Committee on Ending Discrimination against Women, a government decision issued in 2000 lists 456 tasks prohibited to women.

The World Economic Forum's publication, *The Global Gender Gap Report 2015*, based on the country's annual statistics report, documented a widespread gender pay gap and noted that women predominated in low-paying jobs in education, the health-care industry, and low-level sales positions. On average, women earned 38 percent less than men, notwithstanding that 85 percent of women had completed some form of higher education, compared with 68 percent of men.

Persons with disabilities were subject to employment discrimination. Companies with 35 to 100 employees have an employment quota of 1 to 3 percent, while those with more than 100 employees have a 2 to 4 percent quota. The penalty for failure to honor quotas, if enforced, was a fine of 5,000 to 10,000 rubles ($75 to $150), which was insufficient to deter violations. Some local authorities and private employers continued to discourage persons with disabilities from working. Inadequate workplace access for handicapped persons limited their work opportunities.

Indigenous persons faced employment discrimination. Those employed at schools or in local governments felt pressure not to engage in political activism, fearing they could lose their jobs for doing so. Many migrants regularly faced discrimination and hazardous or exploitative working conditions.

Employment discrimination based on sexual orientation and gender identity was a problem, especially in the public sector and education. Employers fired LGBTI persons for their sexual orientation, gender identity, or public activism in support of LGBTI rights. If they expected to be fired, some LGBTI persons chose to resign preemptively to avoid having their future prospects hindered by a dismissal on their resumes. Primary and secondary school teachers were often the targets of such pressure, due to the law's focus on so-called propaganda targeted at minors (see also section 6, Acts of Violence, Discrimination, and Other Abuses Based on Sexual Orientation and Gender Identity).

In Sakhalin a teacher was fired after protecting LGBTI students from harassment. During the year another instructor, Olesya Morozova, was fired from the Shakhtersk Mining College for "committing an immoral act against her students," although the decision appears to have been precipitated by the teacher's effort to protect two LGBTI students from humiliation and physical violence, according to media reports in May. Morozova asserted the college's administrators knew about the harassment against students, which she claimed the school's administrators had encouraged. She reportedly asked local law enforcement authorities to investigate what happened at the college and to clear her of wrongdoing.

Persons with HIV/AIDS were prohibited from working in some areas of medical research and medicine.

e. Acceptable Conditions of Work

The national minimum wage for all sectors was 5,965 rubles ($89) per month, which was 60 percent of the subsistence minimum. The subsistence minimum income used by the government as the official poverty line was 9,500 rubles ($142) per month as of the end of 2015. The portion of the population living below the subsistence minimum in 2015 increased to 13 percent of the population from 11 percent in 2014.

The labor code contains provisions for standard workhours, overtime, and annual leave. The standard workweek cannot exceed 40 hours. Employers may not request overtime work from pregnant women, workers under the age of 18, and other categories of employees specified by federal laws. Standard annual paid leave is 28 calendar days. Employees who perform work involving harmful or dangerous labor conditions and employees in the Far North regions receive additional annual paid leave. Organizations have discretion to grant additional leave to employees.

The labor code stipulates that payment for overtime must be at least 150 percent for the first two hours and not less than 200 percent after that. At an employee's request, overtime may be compensated by additional holiday leave. Overtime work cannot exceed four hours in a two-day period or 120 hours in a year for each employee. The law establishes minimum conditions for workplace safety and worker health but does not explicitly allow workers to remove themselves from hazardous workplaces without threat to their employment. The law entitles foreigners working legally in the country to the same rights and protections as citizens.

Nonpayment of wages is treated as a criminal offense and is punishable by fines, compulsory labor, or imprisonment. The threshold for a criminal offense is partial nonpayment (that is, nonpayment of more than half of an employee's wages) for three months or complete nonpayment for two months. Aggravated offenses could potentially be punished by two to five years' imprisonment and a fine of 50,000 rubles ($750). The government did not effectively enforce the law in either the formal or informal sectors, and nonpayment of wages remained widespread. On July 3, President Putin signed a federal law increasing administrative fines on employers who failed to pay salaries to their employees (wage arrears). The law increased penalties for repeat violators from 50,000 rubles ($750) to 100,000 rubles ($1,500). The law also introduces a progressive scale of compensation to the affected worker(s), paid by the employer. The law became effective on October 1.

An example of nonpayment of wages occurred in November in Novotroitsk, Chelyabinsk region, where construction workers claimed wage arrears totaling 1.7 million rubles ($25,000). They threatened to go on a hunger if they were not paid their back wages. The governor of Orenburg region finally intervened in the case, and all wage arrears were paid.

From January to September, the Prosecutor General's Office identified 555,924 violations involving wage payments by employers. Formal charges were filed in slightly fewer than half of these cases (272,455), while the remainder were dismissed. More than 40,000 persons were detained for violations of disciplinary or administrative regulations/laws.

Serious breaches of occupational safety and health provisions are also criminal offenses. Experts generally pointed to prevention of these offenses, rather than adequacy of the available punishment, as the main challenge to worker rights' protection in these areas. RosTrud, the agency that enforced these provisions, noted state labor inspections were understaffed and that inspectors needed additional professional training. According to official reporting from RosTrud, inspectors found 578,000 labor law violations in 2015. The agency did not provide data on the number of inspectors or budgetary and other resources allocated to enforcement of wage, hour, and occupational safety and health laws. There was no national information available on the number of workplace accidents, fatalities, or deaths during the year. According to Rosstat (the country's statistics office), in 2015 some 28,200 workers were injured in industrial accidents, including 1,290 deaths.

Although no official data were available, experts estimated the workforce in the informal economy was 25 to 30 percent of the total labor force and growing. The largest share of laborers in the informal economy was concentrated in the trade, construction, and agricultural sectors, where workers were more vulnerable to exploitative working conditions. Labor migrants worked in low-quality jobs in construction but also in housing, utilities, agriculture, and retail trade sectors, often informally.

According the most recent information available, GAMI/the FMS reported more than two million undocumented labor migrants in 2015, compared more than four million in 2014. The decline was widely attributed to the country's 23-month recession, which reduced migrant flows to the country, and to penalties for violating migrant labor registration requirements. According to the most recent Rosstat data, as of the first quarter of the year, the country had 149,000 foreign workers with work permits (visa countries) and 1,627,000 foreign workers who had "patents" (from visa-free countries, primarily Uzbekistan, Tajikistan, and Ukraine).

In January 2015 rules came into effect that toughened punishments for foreigners who commit administrative violations. Under the rules authorities may prohibit persons who exceed their officially registered stay in the country by more than a year from entering the country for 10 years. GAMI/the FMS estimated that more than three million persons could be subject to such prohibitions.

In 2015 some 481,404 foreigners, including migrant laborers, were prohibited from entering the country, compared with 682,893 in 2014.

9 781976 379208